To Build a Trail is t... the richly layered e... best way, and, as a ... words on education. ... simply remarkable.

...g: ...e ...e ...e ... ... the *Trail* Paul built. It's

—LESLIE LEYLAND FIELDS, author of *Crossing the Waters* and *The Spirit of Food*

Building a trail—clearing away underbrush, heaving rocks, making room for meanders—was a task Paul Willis set himself in a time of personal sorrow when he needed just such strenuous solitude. But its purpose widened over time: it provided a refuge for others who needed a wild place and an hour of renewal. In this book he has accomplished something similar: a record of his own peregrinations on campus and in classrooms and in the mountains he loves that opens also for readers rich opportunities for personal reflection. The humor, humility, edgy intelligence, and deep reflection that inform the writings gathered here give scope and substance to the words he chose as titles for its four sections: curiosity, love, wonder, and gratitude. Here is a book to be savored, like a slow walk among the oaks.

—MARILYN MCENTYRE, author of *Caring for Words in a Culture of Lies, Word by Word,* and *Make a List: How a Simple Practice Can Change Our Lives and Open Our Hearts*

Paul Willis is one of the few writers who make me laugh out loud. And, at the same time, require me to think. With just enough feeling thrown in to move me without making me weepy. I feel myself in the illuminating presence of a kindred spirit. These essays, drawn directly from the details of his life, prove what we learn from all genres of literature, including the memoir: each person's story has the potential to be our story too.

—DANIEL TAYLOR, author of the Jon Mote novels: *Death Comes for the Deconstructionist* and *Do We Not Bleed?*

Reading these essays, I found a remarkable confidant. Paul Willis takes his readers with him as he climbs in the Sierra Nevada, loses a house to California wildfires, leads a college-level poetry class, and hacks a trail through California wilderness to build a neighborhood gathering-place. I came to depend on his intelligence, his resistance to misplaced authority, and his honest, often funny voice. I think you will too.

—**JEANNE MURRAY WALKER,** author of *Helping the Morning: New and Selected Poems*

Sharp-eyed, tender, blunt, generous, droll, impatient with cant, able to live with uncertainty, and constitutionally incapable of huffing and puffing, Paul Willis is a boon companion in these delicious essays.

— **JOHN WILSON,** editor of *Books & Culture* (1995-2016)

To Build a Trail

To Build a Trail

ESSAYS ON CURIOSITY, LOVE & WONDER

Paul J. Willis

WordFarm

SEATTLE, WASHINGTON

WordFarm
334 Lakeside Ave S, #207
Seattle, WA 98144
www.wordfarm.net

Copyright © 2018 by Paul J. Willis

No part of this publication may be reproduced, stored in a retrieval system or transmitted in any form or by any means, electronic, mechanical, photocopying, recording or otherwise, without the prior permission of WordFarm. All rights reserved with these exceptions:

The poem "Salvatore" (p. 29), is from *Getting to Gardisky Lake* by Paul J. Willis (Nacogdoches, TX: Stephen F. Austin State University Press). Copyright © 2016 by Paul J. Willis. Used by permission.

The poems "Assessment" (p. 105), "Lost and Found" (p. 82), "FDNY" (p. 123), and On the 225th Year of Mission Santa Barbara" (p. 125) are from *Say This Prayer into the Past* by Paul J. Willis (Eugene, OR: Cascade Books). Copyright © 2013 by Paul J. Willis. Used by permission of Wipf and Stock Publishers.

The excerpt from "A Going" (p. 152) is from *Like a Straw Bird It Follows Me, and Other Poems* by Ghassan Zaqtan, translated by Fady Joudah (New Haven, CT: Yale University Press). Copyright © 2012 by Yale University Press. Translation copyright © 2012 by Fady Joudah. Originally published in *Like a Straw Bird It Follows Me* (Beirut, Lebanon: Riad El-Rayyes Books). Copyright © 2008 by Ghassan Zaqtan. Used by permission.

The excerpt from "Atlas" (p. 153) is from *The Earth in the Attic* by Fady Joudah (New Haven, CT: Yale University Press). Copyright © 2008 by Fady Joudah. Used by permission.

USA ISBN-13: 978-1-60226-020-7
USA ISBN-10: 1-60226-020-6
Printed in the United States of America
First Edition: 2018

Library of Congress Cataloging-in-Publication Data
Names: Willis, Paul J., 1955-
Title: To build a trail : essays on curiosity, love, and wonder / Paul J. Willis.
Other titles: Essays on curiosity, love, and wonder
Description: Seattle, WA : WordFarm, 2018. | Includes bibliographical references.
Identifiers: LCCN 2017058292 (print) | LCCN 2018001529 (ebook) | ISBN 9781602260207 (pbk.) | ISBN 1602260206 (pbk.) | ISBN 9781602264274 (ebook) | ISBN 1602264279 (ebook)
Subjects: LCSH: Willis, Paul J., 1955- | Life cycle, Human. | Life change events. | Self-realization. | College teachers--United States--Biography. | Poets, American--California--Biography.
Classification: LCC PS3573.I456555 Z46 2018 (ebook) | LCC PS3573.I456555 (print) | DDC 818/.5409 [B] --dc23
LC record available at https://lccn.loc.gov/2018001529

P 10 9 8 7 6 5 4 3 2 1
Y 24 23 22 21 20 19 18

TO SHARON

*"I sing of times trans-shifting, and I write
How roses first came red, and lilies white."*

Contents

Into the Wilderness ... 13

I. CURIOSITY

Gumdrops ... 19
The Shirt on Our Backs ... 25
Remembering Those We Forget ... 29
Piano Lessons ... 33
Here, Mr. Hoerth ... 37
Hitchin' a Ride ... 43
Can't You See Lear? ... 49
Epiphany at Patsy Clark's ... 55

II. LOVE

To Build a Trail ... 59
Trail Maintenance ... 69
A Meditation for Ash Wednesday ... 75
Poems Lost, Poems Found ... 79
By Any Other Name ... 85
How Are You, My Friend? ... 89

III. WONDER

The Place ... 95

Assessment 105
A Letter to the Faculty 107
The Sixth Chapter of Acts 111
The Garrison Keillor Koan 115
What's a Laureate to Do? 119

IV. GRATITUDE

My First Summer in the Sierra 129
Three Old Ones 133
A Meditation for Good Friday 141
A Century Past "The Soldier" 145
An Evening with the Palestinian Poets 151
My Date with Mary Oliver 157

Notes 163
Acknowledgments 169
Thanks 171
About the Author 173

*We get no good
By being ungenerous, even to a book,
And calculating profits—so much help
By so much reading. It is rather when
We gloriously forget ourselves and plunge
Soul-forward, headlong, into a book's profound,
Impassioned for its beauty and salt of truth—
'Tis then we get the right good from a book.*

—ELIZABETH BARRETT BROWNING

Into the Wilderness

IN THE COLLEGE WHERE I TEACH there is now an Office of Educational Effectiveness—which, to increase its Orwellian elegance, may as well be called the Office of Efficacious Educational Effectiveness. I have suggested we ban the term *educational effectiveness* and replace it with the word *learning*.

But what do I know?

The administrators in this office are dead set on measuring student learning outcomes, as they call them. As far as I can tell, measurable student learning outcomes are a figment of the utilitarian imagination. But the federal government and our accrediting agency believe in them—they very much believe in them—so we are told that we must believe in them as well. It so happens that the abbreviation for student learning outcome, SLO, is the same as that for a neighboring town, San Luis Obispo. I do believe in San Luis Obispo, so that is a start, I suppose.

I have a tendency to stand up in faculty meetings and start and stammer and blush and say that we are in danger of unweaving the rainbow—that, for all our efforts to quantify them, teaching and learning remain a mysterious art, not an exact science. "I am not data!" I once announced. "My students are not data! I am so tired of hearing about data!" Then there was a long silence, and I was conscious of having said something overwrought and maybe even very stupid.

But this is an issue that does not go away for me. I lie in bed making up speeches to the faculty and administration. One of them goes like this: "Do we want to be a college? Do we want to be a liberal arts college? Do we want to be a Christian liberal arts college? Or do we want to be some junior varsity version of IBM!" (*Thunderous applause.*)

Just recently I had a full year off from teaching, perhaps my last sabbatical before I retire. For several months I served as an artist-in-residence in North Cascades National Park. My whole job there was to hike around and write poems about what I saw—which I did, with abandon. (Your tax dollars at work!) But I also found myself, in between poems, writing and recovering essays that seemed to be about learning—the kinds of learning I have done over a now lengthening lifetime. Some of this learning has happened in the official capacity of student or teacher; some of it on the sly.

None of this learning can tolerate the confines of San Luis Obispo. In some cases it has taken thirty, forty, or fifty years to arrive at a kernel or narrative of halfway decent reflection. I found myself noting in one particular essay that curiosity, love, and wonder always take circuitous paths toward understanding. I have made those circuitous paths quite literal in a Byzantine system of trails that I have built in the wilder parts of our California campus. And curiosity, love, and wonder have become convenient guides on the wandering path of this manuscript. And gratitude appears on the horizon as well—gratitude for new and immeasurable understandings.

David Warren, President of the National Association of Independent Colleges and Universities, recently said, "Why are we letting the data geeks determine how we value an education? It's not a quantifiable product." I copied that quote in an email to our administration and heard back, at length and within thirty minutes, from our president, provost, and associate provost. I must have hit a tender spot.

Where do I come by these convictions? It may not be an accident that I planned this collection of essays while living in a national park. For as long as I can remember, I have been drawn to the presence of mountains and forests. My childhood home in Corvallis, Oregon, was built on the city limits. From our backyard, we looked across a dip of pasture to a tall ridge of Douglas fir in the Coast Range. On summer evenings, fresh winds from the ocean blew through those Doug firs, and I took this as an invitation, sometimes hiking alone for a day or two just to see what was there in the university-owned forest.

In high school my older brother and I began climbing the volcanic peaks of the Cascades, which we could also see from our house, east across the Willamette Valley. Then, in college, we began guiding wilderness trips together in the Sierra Nevada, the Trinity Alps, the Wallowa Mountains—as well as in the Cascade Range. And, eventually, we both became involved in grueling, on-the-ground political efforts to save and preserve wilderness (he to a much greater degree, but I have had a taste of it).

All this must have informed my teaching. I think of a poem, a play, a class as a wilderness area full of unanticipated delights. Recently a friend and I went on a two-week backpack trip without a map, and this suited us just fine. "The freshness, the freedom, the farness," writes Robert Service—"O God! how I'm stuck on it all."

If a classroom is like a wilderness area, I do not want to presume that I know what we will find there together. So I do not like to over-script my syllabi. I especially do not want to be in the fraudulent business of predicting measurable student learning outcomes. The classroom is not a factory—it's a wilderness area. That is the metaphor I carry within me. You can calculate the number of board feet of timber in a forest, but once you have done that, it's no longer a forest—it's a pile of lumber on the ground. We need to step lightly on the path, be alert to what lies in wait beyond every switchback, every silent turn of the page, every hand that is not quite raised.

"Well," I say as a teacher. "Will you look at that . . ."

But to all of you data geeks in the Offices of Efficacious Educational Effectiveness Everywhere, let me say that I am grateful even for you. Were it not for the irritations you daily provide, I might never have ventured quite so consciously upon these musings. (And were it not for the irritations I daily provide to you as well, your own lives would perhaps be much less interesting.) Also, it is just possible that in your feeble heart of hearts you do want people to learn, and that in my febrile heart of hearts I want people to learn too, so we might still have something in common. So, though I refuse to fill out your surveys and chart your charts and graph your graphs, I hope you will accept the outcome of these meandering essays.

In other words, peace be with you.

But also with me.

I. Curiosity

Stories are not multiplication tables, and we relish them for their diverse and unpredictable effects.

—DANIEL TAYLOR

Gumdrops

ONE DAY, IN THE WINTER of my sixth-grade year, our old and discontented teacher, Miss Weir, informed us we would now take out our pencils and each write a story for the *Corvallis Gazette-Times* George Washington's Birthday Tall Tale Contest—though the tales could not be all that tall, given the fact that they had to be fifty words or less. We all knew the one about the cherry tree—but that was true, wasn't it? So we scratched our heads and went to work. Because, according to Miss Weir, there was money to be had if we won. How much, she didn't say.

This is what I wrote:

> One night, a Tory at Yorktown filled American guns with black gumdrops. In the morning, when Washington ordered his men to charge and fire, gumdrops emerged instead of bullets. Greedy British soldiers gobbled them up and fell to the ground with bellyaches. Cornwallis thought his men were dead and surrendered.

It is not hard to guess where this story came from. In grade school I liked to read about the Revolutionary War, and I also liked to eat gumdrops, and they must have given me stomachaches from time to time. So with great imaginative flair I connected these experiences—at the same time finding a way to make the father of our country an accidental pacifist.

    So we turned in our stories, and Miss Weir delivered them to the *Gazette-Times*, and we all promptly forgot about them. Until, just before Washington's birthday, Miss Weir announced to the class right after lunch that I had won the contest. I was filled with amazement and pride, and several days later my prize-winning fiction was published in the newspaper under the title "A Sweet Way to Win a War." Then the United Press International scooped it up and splashed it around the country as filler. And then, according to several neighbors, Paul Harvey himself ended his midday news broadcast with the tale—no doubt adding at the end, as he always did, "And now you know . . . the rest of the story."

    This was 1967. The war in Vietnam was of course well underway. I had only the vaguest ideas about this—or, perhaps, none at all. But our country needed every distraction it could lay its hands on. And I happened to be one of them.

    It wasn't the injustice of the Vietnam War that eventually got my attention, however; it was an injustice that emerged in our very classroom. A few days after my brush with literary fame, I put up my hand and asked Miss Weir, "Isn't there some sort of prize money I'm supposed to be getting?"

    Miss Weir pursed her gravely over-lipsticked lips and said, "The prize for the contest is five dollars. But since your story was part of a class project, I am keeping that money in my desk on behalf of the entire class."

    Then she opened her desk drawer, removed a five-dollar bill, and held it aloft for all to see. And then she put it back. And gave me a glassy stare.

    The classroom got very quiet.

    But out on the playground, the verdict was given. "Miss Weir is being Miss Weird. You got robbed, man."

    Which is how I felt myself. But out of some high-mindedness, gained perhaps in Sunday School at the First Baptist Church, I decided not to complain.

But that didn't make things any better. From that day on, for reasons I have never fathomed, Miss Weir declared war on me. And she wasn't using black gumdrops. No, she used big, fat, red *F*s on my assignments, whenever she could manage them. Outline for a report? *F*. Snowflake design? *F*. Notebook organization? *F*. She couldn't get away with it on spelling tests and math quizzes, since I got most every word and problem right and naturally could prove it. But give her a little wiggle room and she became wicked.

I remember trying to tell my mother that Miss Weir did not like me.

"It can't be that bad," she said.

And then, one day, Miss Weir reported to the class after lunch that someone—and here she paused and looked at me—*someone* had stolen the five-dollar bill from her desk. "Now who might that someone be?" she asked.

Out on the playground, everyone said, "The five dollars is yours to begin with. It wasn't really stealing."

But I hadn't taken it, and said so. Face flaming. Hardly anyone believed me. Least of all, Miss Weir.

How the spring played out I can't recall. Miss Weir must have eventually stopped doling out those *F*s, perhaps because of a clandestine parent-teacher conference. Deep down, my mother may have believed me and done what she could to put a stop to bad behavior.

But the more I thought about Miss Weir, the more I hated her in my heart. I nursed my grudge for a long time. And, finally, vengeance was mine.

My opportunity came almost a year later, when I was in the seventh grade. I had come back to the elementary school on a Saturday morning to watch my younger brother play in a basketball game. The game, I suppose, was not all that interesting—or, perhaps,

I was not all that interested. For, halfway through, I slipped away from the shouts in the gym and tiptoed down a hallway to the classrooms of the upper grades. It was very quiet. I told myself I was just looking, just visiting old haunts. I was so much older now. How interesting to reflect back on former days.

Then I came to the door of Miss Weir's sixth-grade classroom. I turned the knob. It opened. And I went inside. And then I knew why I had come. Holding my breath, I walked to the main blackboard, lifted a piece of chalk from the tray, and proceeded to scrawl, in letters as large as I could manage, WE HATE MISS WEIR. Then, for a stereo effect, I did the same on a second blackboard on the other side of the room. And then, for the *coup de grace*, I opened the door to her private closet behind her desk and took out a soft pair of slippers—the ones she put on at the end of the day when she thought we were not looking. The ones to ease the aches and pains and corns and bunions on her elderly, swollen feet. Then I opened the top drawer of her desk, the drawer that had once held the contested five-dollar bill, and found a box of straight pins for posting bulletin-board displays. I dumped half of the box into the toe of her right slipper and half of the box into the toe of her left—where they couldn't be seen, only felt. Then I put the slippers back in her closet. And snuck back out of the room.

I never heard how Miss Weir took it when she got to her classroom that Monday, so there wasn't much triumph to my private act of vandalism. I could imagine, of course, her astonishment and anger upon seeing those messages on the blackboards. And the sudden pain of merging her toes with all those straight pins later on in the afternoon. But for some reason I didn't like thinking about it. My perfect hate crime gave me very little pleasure. I had told myself I was getting even. But all I got was ashamed.

Now that I am as old as Miss Weir was when she was my teacher, and now that I am a teacher as well, I know how little it takes to become locked in conflict with a colleague or a student for reasons that deepen and multiply in the imagination. I know the twinge of envy that I sometimes feel when a younger friend or protégé wins a prize or writes a poem that surpasses any I might win or write myself. And was that it? Was Miss Weir jealous? Had she entered the contest herself? Had she nurtured aspirations as a writer for many a year—aspirations that never met with recognition?

I will never know, of course. But I do know, finally, like Flannery O'Connor's Misfit, that there is no real pleasure in meanness. At a school in which I used to teach, I once expressed myself in a way that so upset one of our administrators that she checked herself into the hospital for two days.

Maybe she found Miss Weir there too.

In my next life, my better life, I will go and visit them there, and bring them flowers. And gumdrops.

The Shirt on Our Backs

Common Ground

Today I dug an orange tree out of the damp, black earth.
My grandfather bought a grove near Anaheim
at just my age. Like me, he didn't know much.
How'd you learn to grow oranges, Bill?
friends said. *Well,* he said, *I look at what*

my neighbor does, and I just do the opposite.
Up in Oregon, he and his brother discovered
the Willamette River. They were both asleep
on the front of the wagon, the horses stopped,
his brother woke up. *Will,* he said, *am it a river?*

My grandfather, he cooked for the army during the war,
the first one. He flipped the pancakes up the chimney,
they came right back through the window onto the griddle.
In the Depression he worked in a laundry during the night,
struck it rich in pocketknives. My grandfather,

he liked to smoke in his orange grove, as far away
    on the property as he could get from my grandmother,
    who didn't approve of life in general, him in particular.
    Smoking gave him something to feel disapproved for,
    set the world back to rights. Like everyone else,

    my grandfather sold his grove to make room
    for Disneyland. He laughed all the way to the bank,
    bought in town, lived to see his grandsons born
    and died of cancer before anyone wanted him to, absent
    now in the rootless presence of damp, black earth.

Growing up, my brothers and I shared and thus fought over an olive-green wool shirt with clumsy buttons. It was our grandfather's, from the First World War, and thus a prize. But it was also very scratchy, and so more often admired than worn. Also, it was too big for any of us.

Our grandfather was a Fleischman whose parents came from East Prussia, where many of his fifteen brothers and sisters had been born. They emigrated in part to avoid the draft under Bismarck, and now here they were, farming in the Willamette Valley of Oregon, and called up to fight against the speakers of their native tongue. I don't believe our grandfather made it past Fort Lewis, in Washington, mustered in and mustered out before he could be shipped overseas.

Still, the olive-green shirt held a kind of romance for all of us. We put it on to play army in the woods, and later on to backpack in the rain and snow of the Cascades. By the time we were through with it, oversized and scratchy as it may have been, the shirt had become a tattered rag.

I think the shirt also attracted us because we had not really known our grandfather—he died when the oldest of us was not yet five years old. Even so, my earliest memory, before even the age of two, concerns him. In the living room of our grandparents' home in Anaheim, California, our grandfather had a favorite chair—a green stuffed rocker. Dark-green, as I recall, and not over-stuffed but lean and scuffed, with a worn, white doily at the head. During one particular family gathering, he left the room briefly, and I crawled up into the dark-green chair by myself. When he came back, he made a generous to-do about my being in his place, and I became the center not only of his attention but also of the entire room's.

I wonder now if my climbing into my grandfather's chair and my wearing of my grandfather's shirt were each an attempt to become this person who must have been so kind to us all. In her most recent birthday card to me, my 89-year-old aunt wrote that a few days after her father had died, I walked over to that green chair and looked at its emptiness in confusion—and that the sight of this made everyone else very sad.

Knowing him in my bones, then, but not really knowing him, I have been an eager collector of stories about my grandfather. Some of these I put in the poem "Common Ground." The poem begins with an anecdote about his moving to Anaheim to cultivate an orange grove: *"How'd you learn to grow oranges, Bill?* / friends said. *Well,* he said, *I look at what* // *my neighbor does, and I just do the opposite."* So matter-of-fact. So self-effacing. And yet there is a definite self, being asserted.

Long after I wrote this poem, my aunt told me another story. Soon after they had arrived in Anaheim, one Sunday, when the morning service had just let out and people were talking amiably on the steps of the church, a man happened to say he'd heard that up in Portland, they rolled up the sidewalks every evening at six o'clock. "I wouldn't know," my grandfather said. "I was always in bed by then."

Our grandfather had moved to Anaheim because he had married a girl from there, an Urbigkeit, and she had nagged him until he agreed to bring their family out of the rain in Oregon and back to southern California. This was during the Depression, and once they got there the ten-acre orange grove wasn't enough to support them.

So he worked for a laundry during the nights and, in his optimistic way, "struck it rich in pocket knives."

But they didn't completely escape the rain. One winter, the torrents came and the house flooded, and he carried his children, one at a time, waist-deep through the orange grove to higher ground. Perhaps that is the image I like best—a little like those nineteenth-century paintings of Jesus, carrying the lambs in his bosom.

Is it possible that our parents and grandparents still carry us, still enfold us in their arms, long after they're dead and gone? My mother, who made that trip across the brown floodwaters in his embrace, has now crossed that final flood by herself, and sometimes I feel that my brothers and I are left here in the rapids alone, trying to carry the ones who have in turn been entrusted to us. But that grim feeling ignores the fact that in having been carried we still are carried, in memory if not in actual, tangible presence. The olive-green shirt, though worn to rags, still rests upon our shoulders, and the dark-green chair, though empty, is full.

Remembering Those We Forget

Salvatore

It was the mile we ran together.
I had some grace in the way I did it,
or so I imagined, but you
were the angular plodder, always staring
down the lane to where you would be,
following me across the line.

Afterward, nobody spoke to you on the bus—
your thick black hair, your stony face,
your dark shoes big as a circus.
On a back road, we watched you disappear
into an unpainted house with walls
made of rain and blackberry vines.

Senior year, you moved
into an old hotel down by the river.

With some girl. The carpet in the hallway
there was stained with sourness and smoke.
On Christmas Day, I left a red
Swiss Army knife beside your door.

Sal, did I know you? I remember
your hard breathing, just behind
my right shoulder, the inexorable
slap of your feet in those flat
and broken tennis shoes as they cut
at my heels around each bend.

    I began the poem "Salvatore" in a California ranger station at the suggestion of Paulann Petersen, the former poet laureate of Oregon. I had invited her down to Santa Barbara to lead a couple of writing workshops, to give a reading, and to participate in a memorial observance of the poet William Stafford. Stafford served from 1942–46 in a variety of civilian public service camps as a conscientious objector, and two of those years were spent at a camp in the mountains behind Santa Barbara. Every winter, around the time of his birthday, a few of us gather to read some of his poems there, and this time Paulann joined us.

    Bill Stafford was a good friend of hers, and in one of her workshops she used his poems to get us writing our own. The Stafford poem that got mine started was called "At Liberty School." It's a memory poem from his boyhood in Kansas, about a girl in one of his classes that nobody knew very well: "Girl in the front row who had no mother / and went home every day to get supper, / the class became silent when you left early."

    Paulann asked us to think about someone from childhood who essentially went unnoticed, and the person who came to my mind was an awkward Italian boy named Salvatore. I can't remember his last name. I believe his father was a brilliant but poverty-stricken professor at the local university in the Oregon town where I grew up. Salvatore was the opposite of excitable; he was quiet, brooding, and deliberate. We ran track together in high school, and though I was a little bit faster, he was usually right on my shoulder, and we developed a silent sort of companionship. As I look back, however, I wonder, of course, how well I really knew him. My father also taught at the university, but we were not poor, and all of us in our family experienced a basic level of social confidence and social acceptance. For me, it was probably hard to imagine what it was like to be without these gifts of fortune.

William Stafford was also poor (or close to it) when growing up, and moved enough from town to town to often be the new kid on the block. He might have had a greater sensitivity to outcasts than I did. From early on he developed a habit and ethic of "standing with" a person who was bullied or ignored, whether that person was the black elevator man in his poem "Serving with Gideon" or simply a taunted child on the playground. I'm not sure I had that habit, but I think of the poem that I have written about Salvatore as a kind of "standing with" across time. The gesture—or act, if you will—is belated, to be sure, but I hope it is no less genuine, and perhaps, even, in the way that prayer might be, efficacious.

Piano Lessons

I WAS IN HIGH SCHOOL, a sophomore maybe, and had briefly revived an interest in learning to play the piano. Or perhaps my mother had revived it for me—I don't recall. In any case, this was my last grasp at the keyboard. In grade school I had tried and quit, disheartened by a thin, ever-vigilant woman who, when I did not play up to her standards, made me stay after the lesson in a corner of her living room and copy out notes from the masters onto a blank set of staffs. Her masters were people like Mozart, Bach, and Bartók. My mother wanted me to learn to play hymns by Fanny Crosby; she and the teacher not so subtly fought about this.

But now, in high school, a young and lovely pastor's daughter from a neighboring town had moved to ours with her curly-haired Adonis husband. They lived in a falling-down two-story rental across from the church, and every Sunday afternoon I would ride my bike down the hill, knock on their rusted screen door, and repair with her to the sanctuary, where I would practice psalms and hymns and spiritual songs while she sat patiently beside me on the polished wooden bench.

One afternoon—it must have been spring, the warm air laden with blossoms—I banged my bike over curb, mounted the decaying steps, and knocked on the screen door. No one came. But the wooden door behind the screen was wide open, and floating out of the upstairs window over the porch came murmuring, commingled sounds.

"*Oooh*," said the Adonis husband.

"Darling," said she.

I should have left, of course, but this was my appointed hour. People have obligations to meet, I told myself, and I didn't want to pedal my bike back up the hill without a lesson to show for it. So I knocked again—louder this time.

The murmuring from the window ceased.

"Darling, someone's at the door."

"*Oooh*," said her husband.

"Oh, no," said she. "I forgot! The lesson!"

"*Oooh*," said her husband.

"I will come back, I promise," said she. "Darling, I will."

And then she came slipping down the stairs and appeared at the door in all of her raven-haired, disheveled glory, full of the promise of fruition, and I—I had no words at all for the shifting chords beneath my belly. But the pastor's daughter accompanied me that golden, flowery afternoon across the street to the sanctuary, where we sat in the gloom at the dark piano while I stumbled through my thousand tongues, her ripening thigh resting inches from my own, her gaze directed into the far corners of that cavernous room.

I believe that I quit again soon after that, lured away by science and football and snow-capped mountains and the many other things of this world. And was it worth it, the time that I spent with my hands on those keys, the time that I stole from that beautiful couple, so young and so fresh in the bloom of their marriage?

A year or so later, a friend and I found the pastor's daughter completely alone in a backcountry meadow at the foot of Mt. Jefferson. Her husband had ventured onto the peak all by himself, and she was starting to worry about him. "Don't," we said. But I already knew from experience that Mt. Jefferson was a very dangerous peak indeed. He must have made it down safely, though, for we never heard otherwise. But that, I think, was the last time I saw her, a damsel slightly in distress, still lovely as ever, and in need of someone other than me.

Here, Mr. Hoerth

IN THE FALL OF MY FRESHMAN YEAR at Wheaton College in Illinois, I took a required survey of the Old Testament. I would have taken the class anyway, because I hoped to major in biology and biblical studies en route to becoming a doctor on the mission field. In the meantime, however, since I seemed to be spending most of my weekends on rock-climbing trips to Devil's Lake in Wisconsin, I was not passing my calculus class, which did not bode well for my plans to attend medical school. But I did like climbing, and was sincere about biblical study, and I noticed that the Old Testament had a few mountains in it.

The class was taught by a wry and patient man with a small, dark mustache. He told us to call him Mr. Hoerth. Not Professor. Not Doctor. Just Mister. I liked that about him. In response to our questions, he would say things like "I would tell you who it was that Cain married, if I were Abel." He also told us that he was an archaeologist who spent his summers digging around in Israel and Palestine. That the clock tower of Edman Chapel was in fact filled to the brim with potsherds from previous Wheaton expeditions, and if anyone wanted to help him catalog these precious items, we should let him know. To my knowledge, no one volunteered. That red-brick clock tower was pretty massive, and I, for one, could think of better things to do in my spare time—like climb red quartzite in Wisconsin. When Mr. Hoerth would call the roll, I would sometimes cling to the facade of the building under the second-story window until he intoned my name. Then I would clamber over the window ledge and calmly say, "Here, Mr. Hoerth."

We would both keep a straight face. That was the cool thing about it.

A few years later, as a senior, I asked my creative writing teacher to fill me in on graduate school. "Like, how does that work?" I asked.

"I've heard that in the summers you teach climbing in Yosemite," he primly said.

"That's right," I replied, pleased he would know this.

"That's probably a pretty good job for you," he said.

And then he walked off.

But I am getting ahead of myself. As a freshman trudging through autumn leaves on Wheaton sidewalks, miserably aware that the highest point in DuPage County was a landfill called Mount Trashmore, this future insult would have sounded like a blessing. And when we got to the story of Noah in Mr. Hoerth's Old Testament survey, something clicked. Though Mr. Hoerth allowed there might be something mythic, even folklorish, about the flood, the ark, the forty days, he also said that "the mountains of Ararat," where the book of Genesis says the ark came to rest, have often been identified with an actual peak in Armenia in eastern Turkey—a very tall peak at 16,854 feet, its summit draped with glacial ice. Mr. Hoerth added, with a slender smile, that several expeditions had been mounted to discover the remains of the ark, high on the mountain.

That sounded like a pretty good job for me—and I cooked on it for several weeks. Then, at the end of a Friday afternoon class session, I marched up to the lectern and reported for duty. "Mr. Hoerth," I said. "I would like to go on an expedition to find the ark on Mt. Ararat. I've done a good bit of climbing in the Cascades in Oregon, where I grew up, and I just spent my whole summer on the Juneau

Icefield in Alaska, so I know how to use an ice ax and crampons. Really well. I'm even trained in crevasse rescue. So I think they could use me for something like this. Do you know of an expedition that I could go on?"

It would be perfect. At Wheaton College my professors always talked about the integration of faith and learning. Using my exceptional skills honed over the last three years in the mountains of Oregon and Alaska, I was bound to find the remains of the ark deep in the recesses of some glacier, somewhere right next to the summit, since I might as well get to the top while I was at it. The climb would be an apologetic triumph—the truth of the Bible proved beyond a shadow of a doubt—and all because of my steady determination and my handy ice ax, twirling in my dapper grip.

So I was confused when Mr. Hoerth paused before answering me. Then he said, "Well. *Hmmm.*" And then he shook his head slowly, as if clearing it of a few stray potsherds.

"I'll tell you what I'll do," he said finally. "I'll give you a book to read this weekend, and, on Monday, if you still want to go find the ark, I'll connect you with the right people."

"Deal," I said, and shook his hand, though I noticed his grip seemed surprisingly limp.

I walked back with him to his office in Blanchard Hall, the iconic structure of the college, built of Kankakee dolomite, rough to the touch and apparently ideal for climbing but not so when you actually ventured up the face—that dolomite was flaky as Hades. Mr. Hoerth rummaged through his shelves until he found the book he was looking for, then handed it to me with an air of mild distaste. The book's title, in yellow psychedelic letters, was *The Quest for Noah's Ark*. And the book's author, in white print, appropriate for such a knight errant, was John Warwick Montgomery.

"See you Monday," he said.

That weekend I did not go climbing in Wisconsin. I sat high up on a fire escape in balmy weather and read all 335 pages of

John Warwick Montgomery, for in my hands were the keys to the kingdom of my future. There were lots of pictures, and that made the reading go faster. Maps, of course. Charts of previous expeditions. Fuzzy photographs of ark-like shapes in the ice—about as clear as images I had seen of Bigfoot back in Oregon. But most of the images, curiously, were of the author himself. (Or of his son, who apparently had set an altitude record on the mountain for someone of his tender age.) These photographs invariably displayed Dr. Montgomery, all done up in his newly purchased alpine gear, posed on the side of the mountain, ice ax in hand. Most of the captions read something like this: "The author, at 12,000 feet." "The author, at 13,000 feet." "The author, at 14,000 feet." The author may or may not have made it to the top of Mt. Ararat, but that was beside the point. He had heroically made his presence known, and that was sufficiently impressed on his readers.

But to my further surprise, I was not sufficiently impressed with his apologetics. Because Jesus had once said "As it was in the days of Noah, so shall it be also in the days of the Son of Man," it was of paramount importance, said Dr. Montgomery, that the ark be found. And once the ark was found, he said, everyone on earth would be absolutely compelled to believe in Jesus. So by finding the ark, he would be bringing about the salvation of the entire world.

Whoa, I thought. *Seriously?*

He could of course have argued something much more nuanced than this; memory dims and simplifies. But this is what I remember, and this is what I remember turning away from. And those endless snapshots of the author striking a pose with his ice ax (which I may have multiplied in memory)—they were of course pictures of me. Like the rich young ruler, I climbed down from that fire escape and went away sorrowfully. It is hard to abandon a cherished vision of your once and future self, even if that self has been reflected back in a funhouse mirror.

On Monday afternoon, after class, I returned the book to Mr.

Hoerth.

"Well?" he said.

I hesitated.

"I don't think it's for me," I said. "This ark stuff. I think I'll be staying here, Mr. Hoerth. Right here."

Hitchin' a Ride

ONE SATURDAY AFTERNOON DURING THE SPRING of my freshman year at Wheaton, I sat in the college library while the sun shone and the day wasted, trying to catch up on my homework. It had been a long winter in the dreary suburbs of Chicago, and I was restless. In the next carrel over was a fellow freshman named Scott Loizeaux—equally restless, I could tell, from the sewing-machine bounce of his leg.

That's when I had an idea.

"Hey, Scott," I said. "I've got a really good friend from home who's at Valparaiso University. Just over the state line. Couldn't be more than sixty miles as the crow flies. I bet we could hitchhike there by dark. Whaddya say?"

"I say let's do it," Scott said.

I was surprised that he didn't need more persuading. But now that Scott had agreed to the plan, I felt it would be impolite to abandon it. So we dumped our books, found our jackets, and rustled up a highway map of the area. A direct route would take us through Chicago Heights on the South Side, but that meant nothing to us. I came from a small town in Oregon, and Scott was an eager missionary kid from Panama—a couple of young white boys who were basically not from here. Chicago Heights sounded like any other American suburb—maybe more upscale than most.

We walked past the edge of our red-brick college town, thumbs out, into a swath of farmland. The birds were singing, the trees were greening, the air was breezing, and we congratulated ourselves on leaving the library behind. Before long, a station wagon pulled over, and a middle-aged white fellow—very tidy in appearance—invited us along with him. He was doing some errands, happy to help us on our way, and spoke about getting home to his wife in time for dinner and then getting ready for Sunday School the following morning. By the time our roads diverged and he let us out, Scott and I were filled with pity for his unadventurous life.

Still in farmland, we walked along in the now latening afternoon and were soon rewarded with another ride—this one in a dark, two-door sedan. A pair of jolly Hispanic men in dirt-stained clothes occupied the front seat, and Scott and I crawled into the back. Note to future hitchhikers: think twice before you get in the back of a two-door sedan. For after we had tucked ourselves in and were underway, we began to realize our chaperones were a bit sloppy, talking louder than need be and gesturing emphatically. Alcohol was in the air. How much they'd had, we couldn't tell.

The farmland gave way, and we seemed to be getting into the South Side of Chicago, driving now on city streets. Except our driver was still going at highway speeds. Scott and I exchanged a very grim glance and hung on to the armrests. Since both doors were in the front, there was no chance of abandoning ship, even at a stoplight.

So at last I leaned forward and said, "You can let us out right here, actually." I tried to sound cheerful about it.

The driver turned completely around, taking his eyes off the road. "Don't worry, gringo!" he shouted, waving his arm magnanimously. "We get you there!"

Then he drove even faster, and started to weave in and out of city traffic. Suddenly we were missing our tidy man from the farmlands. Our tidy whitey. Before long, however, there were red and blue flashing lights right behind us, sirens too. Our driver, bless his suddenly law-abiding heart, pulled the sedan to the curb, and a pair of policemen hauled us onto the sidewalk. White policemen. Irish, maybe. They shoved the two Hispanic guys down onto the hood of the car. Then one of the officers cocked his beefy head our way, eyebrows raised.

"And you?" he said.

"*Um*, we were just hitchhiking," I replied. "Can we, like, leave?"

The cop looked us up and down, as if trying to decide whether to book us for that very offense. Then he said, "Get out of here."

So we did. It was getting toward dusk by now, and we walked for a long time. According to a sign we passed, we were finally in Chicago Heights. For a place that sounded like a ritzy suburb, Chicago Heights looked pretty beat up. As in, completely decayed. Paint peeling. Rusted. Askew. Falling down. Graffiti-laden.

The streets became narrow, and as night came on, we noticed lots of African American men standing in the dark of the doorways on the sidewalk. Some had vacant, glassy eyes. Others gave us a hard stare as we passed by, as if we didn't belong here, as if we were trespassing on their turf. Then some of them started to flip us the bird and tell us white boys what we could go do to ourselves. Their muttering joined in a hectic chorus, doorway after doorway. It may have been as harmless as the infield chatter on a Little League baseball diamond—but to us it sounded like the buzz of rattlesnakes on a desert trail. Now, of course, we really missed our tidy whitey. Getting ready for Sunday School sounded like a great idea, a privilege, a luxury.

And then, thanks be, a black van pulled up to the curb, and its door slid open, releasing an almost visceral blast of hard rock. A gaggle of faces urged us in. White faces, young faces, just like ours. No doubt about it—we were saved.

Without a moment's hesitation, Scott and I dove inside onto a shag rug in the back. The door closed. No windows. The bass pumping through the speakers into our ears. A bit claustrophobic, but who cared? We sprawled on that shag rug in relief, and the van took off, coursing through the narrow streets.

After a little while, though, we noticed that our genial hosts were not paying us much attention. All five or six of them were leaning together around the console at the front, discussing something pretty intently. One of them glanced back at us from time to time, as if trying to determine what we were worth.

Then he decided to clue us in.

"This guy from another gang," he said, "he killed one of our guys last week. So we're figuring out how to shoot one of their guys. Tonight."

I saw Scott's eyes grow wide. I'm sure mine did too. But we both nodded back politely as if to say, *Hey, well, if we have any good ideas, we'll just pitch in with the planning, okay? Maybe put us on the refreshments committee?*

They must have sensed right then that we wouldn't be much help, for they dumped us at the next corner.

By now it was completely dark.

We were still in Chicago Heights.

And a youth pastor of our own now-tainted race, angel of mercy that he was, spotted us trembling on that corner and drove us all the way out of town to the Indiana cornfields. There we waited at a McDonalds and very meekly called my friend to pick us up. Eventually—midnight, maybe—we made it to the celestial city of Valparaiso.

So, what is the moral to this story? That it's better to stay in the library on a Saturday afternoon? That if you are going to hitchhike, you should, like the Music Man, at least know the territory? That drunk drivers are likely to be generous, and that generous people can kill you? That just when you think it's people of another race who might hurt you, you find out it's people of your own race who might be the most lethal of all? That God sent that youth pastor to save our skins so that we might be preserved until this very day to do his bidding?

Could be any of these things. Or none. In the midst of the murderous violence that greeted the Civil Rights movement, when asked to sum up the core of the gospel, Will Campbell famously said, "We're all bastards, but God loves us anyway." But to sum up that afternoon and evening with Scott—that strange cocktail of innocence, prejudice, paranoia, and, perhaps, actual threat—I'm tempted simply to say, "We were both stupid, but we got lucky." Divine luck. Let's hope.

Can't You See Lear?

IN MY JUNIOR YEAR I TOOK a required literature class at Wheaton College. I had just dropped my major in biology and was trying to recover some old interests. My father was a biologist, but I did not seem to be destined to follow in his footsteps. I also had a major going in biblical studies, but it was likewise clear to me that I wasn't much of a theologian. So literature might be me, I thought. After all, I had a habit of writing short stories when I should have been memorizing the Krebs cycle or rehearsing the points of the endless debate between Calvin and Arminius.

This literature class was taught by Dr. Beatrice Batson, the chair of the English Department. She was formal, passionate, and severe in a way that I did not understand. For her, each work of literature seemed to be a clear matter of life and death. We read the English devotional poets John Donne and George Herbert, the Russian novelist Fyodor Dostoevsky, and, of course, Shakespeare. I hadn't read Shakespeare since *Romeo and Juliet* in the ninth grade.

King Lear was our chosen play, and Dr. Batson unleashed her full fury of declamation upon the text—and upon us, her confused and frightened students. Halfway through the play, King Lear gets shut out in a cruel storm by his heartless daughters and rages on in sheer madness for pages and pages on the heath. "Class!" Dr. Batson would cry. "Come with me, class! Can't you see Lear lying on the ground? Can't you see him? So old, so suffering, so confused? Oh, the wind, the rain, the agony of it all!"

We would stare back at her blankly, or down at the sunlit floor, a little embarrassed. As for me, I really didn't see or feel any of it. What I remember thinking, in fact, is that King Lear should simply receive Jesus Christ as his personal savior, stop moaning, and get on with his sorry life. Up to that point in my own fairly sheltered existence, I think I had been protected from personal tragedy. Though that would soon change.

The next quarter, I left college to join a climbing expedition to what was then called Mt. McKinley in Alaska. It was a climb that began in high spirits and ended about a month later in disaster. We did not quite reach the top, and two of our members—one of them my own brother—lost most of their hands and feet to frostbite. When I got back to school I thought I could begin to see King Lear in his agony. I did not become an English major, but literature began to feel more adequate than anything else to name the suffering I now knew, and that is the direction I headed in graduate school, with Dr. Batson and her voice in the echoing forefront of my mind.

In graduate school, at Washington State University, my background in literature was so poor that I had to start with an undergraduate Shakespeare course. I very dutifully did so, with Dr. John Wasson, and before too many years went by I ended up writing a dissertation on Shakespeare—something about the way he uses forest settings in his plays. In retrospect, the topic didn't matter much. What mattered was my immersion for several years in that language, in those plays. That dissertation, I now realize, was written in something pretty close to iambic pentameter.

Degree in hand, I then taught for three years at Houghton College in New York. At the time I wondered what kind of writer I would become. In graduate school I had also drafted an eco-fantasy novel with a Shakespearean title, *No Clock in the Forest*. Would

I become a scholar, like Dr. Wasson, who combed the records of manor houses in England for shillings paid to visiting companies of actors? Would I become a novelist, like Madeleine L'Engle, who often showed up at Wheaton College and told us that *A Wrinkle in Time* had been rejected thirty-nine times? Or would I be both, like C. S. Lewis, and also become a highly sought-after chapel speaker in the bargain?

As it turned out, I became none of these things. I did publish that novel and several sequels. And I did write a scholarly article or two. And I did make an appearance in chapel now and again. But at Houghton I started having breakfast once a week with two of my colleagues, Jack Leax and Jim Zoller, and they were poets. They didn't exactly encourage me to write my own poems as well, but looking over their shoulders, I decided to try. And thirty years later, I am still trying.

Then, at Westmont College, where I have spent most of those thirty years, a cherished colleague, Heather Speirs, told me one day as we sat on a bench that I should not overlook the personal essay. It came as a revelation. Something right under my nose—the kind of thing I had been assigning to students and on occasion writing myself—could, in fact, be its own legitimate art form.

No previous effort is lost in the divine economy of our lives. Most of my poems seem to be biblically informed meditations on things like poison oak and red-flowered elderberry—so there are my abandoned majors, still with me. Once in a while someone throws me a compliment on the narrative quality of these poems—something that I must have learned while drafting that series of novels. Or someone has a kind word about a certain lyrical moment in an essay—an inheritance from the writing of poems. When I think about it, the whole unlikely progression makes me laugh.

Other writers have meandered and doubled back in similar ways. I have a hunch that Shakespeare himself wanted to be a poet more than anything else. After his first few years as a playwright, the theaters were closed by the plague. This is when he most certainly wrote his two long narrative poems, *Venus and Adonis* and *The Rape of Lucrece*, and when he most probably wrote his *Sonnets*, sprinkled with embarrassed references to the stage. To be a poet with a patron was a time-honored profession; to be a man of the theater was to be little more than a vagabond. But the plague ended, patronage was not paying the bills, and Shakespeare went back to the boards, turning out the most purely lyrical plays he ever composed: *Romeo and Juliet*, *Midsummer Night's Dream*, and *Richard II*. Throughout his life, Shakespeare wrote far more poetically than need be to keep the attention of a theater audience. His financial failure as a poet made him a playwright for all time.

For an opposite example, take Robert Browning in the Victorian era, who also began his career as a playwright in London. In those days a play would last on the stage for as long as people were willing to see it; his typically lasted for a single night, maybe two. After eloping to Italy with Elizabeth Barrett, there was no reason for him to continue to write plays in English. So he turned to a genre he had always loved, poetry, and made himself famous through the perfection of a kind of poem known as the dramatic monologue, in which character after character speaks convincingly, without interruption, from the page. "My Last Duchess" and her many exquisite cousins would never have existed without Robert Browning's years of failure as a playwright.

And the examples go on. James Joyce wanted to be a poet. William Faulkner wanted to be a poet. Even C. S. Lewis very badly wanted to be a poet—and for all of his many talents, poetry turned out to be the least of his gifts. Unlike Joyce and Faulkner, Lewis did not so much excel in fiction as in nonfiction—and the core strength of his essays are his sudden, sparkling analogies that clinch the argument every time. And what is an analogy but a rationally dressed-up metaphor? And where does one learn metaphor but in the writing of poetry?

Our dead ends are but open doors, each one no more inviting than the eye of a needle. We pass through like kidney stones, with pain and peril, each step an apparent catastrophe. Lear in the storm loses his foolish dreams of himself to find another way of speaking. It's worth it, of course. But the wind, the rain, the agony of it all!

Epiphany at Patsy Clark's

BACK WHEN MY WIFE AND I WERE IN SCHOOL, up the street from our blonde-brick apartment house was a mansion-restaurant, Patsy Clark's. It was made of rich, orange sandstone that had been imported from Morocco before the turn of the last century. Patsy Clark's had green gargoyles and airy balconies. Inside, chandeliers burned deep into the night. In front, two girls in green knickers stood coyly by the double doors, waiting to greet the elect. We often strolled by in the evening, but couldn't afford to eat there.

There was an old man in our neighborhood who searched the alleys for aluminum cans. His name was Dick. He walked softly and carried a big stick, which he used to stir the contents of our green dumpster. Sometimes he used the stick to direct imaginary traffic. Someone had given him a digital watch, but he didn't know how to work it. He asked me once how to work his watch. I didn't know either.

Dick was easy to spot from a distance because he never took three steps without spinning completely around—always to the left, counterclockwise. If we were close enough, we could hear his gunny sack of aluminum cans clank on his hip as he made his many pirouettes. I often wondered why he did this. I know now that it was Tourette's syndrome. But my theory then was that once, long ago, someone had surprised him from the left side. It would never happen again.

In the apartment below us lived a young ballet dancer. Her name was Pam. She had very graceful Chinese features and addressed her mail in elegant script. Newspaper photos caught her in striking poses. She must have practiced her ballet constantly, for we saw her seldom.

One night, however, I awoke to a full moon and saw her dancing outside our window. Dick was dancing with her. Their sacks of aluminum cans clashed like cymbals in the air, and they whirled down the walk in fits of silent mirth. The big stick flew upwards like a magic wand, and they took turns catching it on the twirl. The digital watch slipped unnoticed through the air and shattered on the street. I saw them spin away, leaping nimbly over parked cars, until they reached the shining entrance of Patsy Clark's, where the girls in green knickers sang heavenly alleluias as they opened wide the doors.

It would never happen again.

II. Love

*Poetry is a response to the daily necessity
of getting the world right.*

—WALLACE STEVENS

To Build a Trail

"[S]he being dead yet speaketh."

THOUGH I DIDN'T DISAPPEAR with a shovel into the woods until the first week of June, I think now that it started when my mother died in April. Hers was a lingering death from cancer in her abdomen. After nearly a year of ineffectual surgery and treatment, she was put under hospice care and lasted for another month of morphine and popsicles (mostly grape). She and my father lived in a comfortable retirement center near Portland, Oregon, almost a thousand miles north of my current home in Santa Barbara. I was able to be with them for the first two weeks of hospice care. Then I had to get on a plane and resume my neglected classes.

Leaving my mother as she lay dying seems to me the most cruel and arbitrary thing that I have ever had to do. I bowed my head and sobbed, and she roused herself and stroked my hair. Not very coherent in her last days, she managed to pull her thoughts together for some earnest words of parting. "I have given all of you boys, each one of you, to the Lord," she said. "And I have lived to see Him give each one of you a purpose."

Now that I reflect on her words, I see how much they are part of her, a woman of faith and a woman of duty. A year or two ago, at an English Department potluck, we played a spontaneous parlor game that arose from a question. "When you hear your mother speaking to you in the back of your mind," someone asked, "what is she saying?" I knew immediately. The voice in my head says, "Doesn't it feel good to have your work done?"

In those weeks with my parents in Oregon, I spent an hour or two every day on a stack of essays and exams that I had brought along with me. And almost every day as well, my mother would ask if I had finished grading my papers. Each time, I had to say that I was making progress, but there were still more to read. "You better get going on those," she would say.

A few days before I left, I told her that I had marked 85 papers so far and had only 16 more to go.

"That's terrible," she slurred.

"What's terrible?" I asked. "That I have so much work at the college?"

"No," she said. "Sixteen. That's too many. You need to get those done."

In some ways I may have disappointed my mother. I never became the missionary she herself once hoped to be, or the church organizer that she most certainly was. And my short stints as a department chair have routinely ended in frustration. My repeated attempts to cut back on administrative responsibilities to spend a little more time on my writing were only met by her incomprehension. "Don't you want to be in the know?" she would say. Or, "I can't understand why you wouldn't want to be in charge of that program. It helps so many people, and when you think about it, your writing is only for yourself."

But I have not disappointed my mother in that I have become, like her, a very faithful doer of tasks. When I played high-school football, my coach had a nickname for me: "Hardworking Willis." The name embarrassed me somewhat, but I'm guessing that my mother was in love with it. "Hardworking" identified the person she wanted me to become, the one who ran every sprint at the end of practice as hard as he could. Not faster than others—just harder.

My mother's memorial service took place during finals week of spring semester. Then came a flurry of grading, and after that an ill-timed reading tour to colleges in the Northwest. When I arrived home near the end of May, I was not eager to dive into the writing projects that normally make my summers so enjoyable. Instead of hunkering down at the computer, I read novels. I walked the dog. I sat with my wife and son and daughter whenever I could, and listened, and talked. But I wasn't writing. And I couldn't get used to the fact that my mother was dead.

That's when it occurred to me to scout out some overgrown fragments of trail that led up a little canyon above our house on land that belonged to the college. It had been a wet winter in our part of California: the browning thistles were head high and the poison oak was luxuriant. The isolated remnants of path were wildly impassable, the links between them located only in my imagination. Thrashing through the brush, however, I thought I saw a way.

So one evening in early June, I put on long sleeves and long pants; gloved up; grabbed shovel, hoe, rake, loppers, shears, clippers, and tree saw; borrowed a large wheelbarrow from under the redwood baseball stands; and headed through a screen of laurel and acacia into a stand of eucalyptus. After a bit of trial and error, I developed certain habits and methods that varied with the territory. There in the woods, the first order of business was to cut away dead limbs at eye level, then to dig up the worst of the poison oak. I soon learned that the poison oak had thick, continuous root systems. They could be arbitrarily cut off but never completely pulled out. I tried to keep the shining tangles of roots and vines and Trinitarian glabrous leaves at a shovel-handle's distance, but after a while I grew careless, and a few days later the flesh on the inside of my wrists was the first to know it.

But I was getting somewhere. Branches and shrubbery out of the way, the next step was to pull away the herbs and leaves and duff and detritus—anything that could be raked off or tossed aside. Then came the shovel work, digging up the more stubborn roots and shaping the trail to the terrain, carving it into the side of a slope where necessary, sometimes even cutting steps in a steep bank that didn't allow for a switchback. Boulders had to be rolled out of the way in places, then rolled back to shore up narrow sections of loose trail. There was also garbage to put in the wheelbarrow, and plenty of it: cans, bottles, tires, chairs, batteries, buckets, baseballs, condoms—even a rusty bedspring and mattress. My favorite find was an ancient flask of cinnamon schnapps, distilled in St. Paul, Minnesota.

But I am getting ahead of myself. That first evening I cut the trail in a sinuous line that dipped through the poison oak and eucalyptus near the creek and then climbed into a border of live oak. Because of the deep tree cover, the undergrowth was not terribly thick there. And so I was able to rough out perhaps a couple hundred feet before stopping at dusk on the edge of a field, just where the branches of oak framed the tall, yellowing grass. This felt satisfying—not just the work, but this particular pausing place. A friend once told me that most primitive campsites in Africa are found where forest meets savannah. This is where hunters could see their prey without being seen in return. And this practical preference has apparently been translated over the years into an aesthetic one. Think of the landscape paintings of Constable and Turner, or those of the Hudson River School. Safely embowered under the spreading chestnut tree, we gaze out under arch of bough to open lands that verge upon terrestrial infinity. I had arrived with my nascent trail at this archetypal place. And then I walked toward home through another, the darkening woods that I now safely navigated on a dirt path which my feet could feel better than my eyes could see. I emerged from the trees by the baseball diamond and returned the trusty wheelbarrow with the firm feeling that I would be back.

And I did come back, whenever I could, off and on for two months, until I had crafted a trail that stretched a half mile up the canyon to a road that marked the upper end of the land owned by the college. There were trials and tribulations, of course. Brambles and thistles by the acre, downed trees, and twining stocks of poison oak as thick as my now-oozing wrists. But day after day I awoke before dawn with a quiet excitement and wheeled my tools into the forest at first light on a lengthening path that tangibly measured my progress. The Santa Barbara morning fog created a quiet and coolness about me. The fog might linger until the early afternoon, and sometimes I kept at it for that long, pausing only to sit on the ground with a water bottle and candy bar, watching the lizards do their push-ups.

The work was interrupted twice by trips into the High Sierra, the kind I would normally dream about for weeks and months ahead of time and then recount *ad nauseam* to anyone willing to listen. But on each of these hikes into stunningly pristine alpine country, havens of rock and snow and sky, I often lay awake at night thinking about the next section of trail to clear in the lowly *barranca* near my home. I thought about it the way I would normally think about a peak I especially wanted to climb. And I did climb some of those on my two trips—Humphreys, Darwin, Julius Caesar—but as much as I enjoyed these mountains, something in me wanted to exchange my ice ax for a shovel.

From time to time, one of my colleagues would chance on the trail, such as it was thus far, and offer to help. As much as I appreciated their interest and generosity, I gradually came to realize that I wanted to do this by myself, the same way I could only imagine writing a novel by myself. I was going to say *writing a poem*, since I haven't tackled a novel in a good while, but making a trail is much more like conceiving a long narrative line. A trail has plot, and progress, and duration. It is more than a few metaphors: it is a journey over time. And, as in the writing of a novel, whole chapters sometimes have to be scrapped. Early on, I abandoned and covered up a hastily built section of trail to reroute it in a more pleasing place, dropping down below a row of eucalyptus to stay out of sight of a couple of outlying Quonset huts. Higher up, I inadvertently threw a switchback onto the property of a neighbor of the college. He was nice about it, but also firm: for the sake of liability, he didn't want this trail on his land. So I promptly rerouted that bend in the path, making it unavoidably shorter and steeper in the process. It is passable, this newer way, but I look at that old switchback with longing. My original line was much gentler, and much more artful in its curve. I think of it in the way I think of some favorite passage of mine that some not-so-favorite editor has done away with.

So trail-making is like writing, which, for me, is not a very collaborative process. But I also suspect that making this trail has been a very personal task in more than just a writerly fashion. I wonder now if I have been doing the work of grief, if I have been making literal what each of us is always doing, all of the time, but especially in a time of loss: clearing a new path for ourselves, making a way, finding direction. At the beginning of *The Divine Comedy*, Dante's pilgrim finds himself in the dark wood, the *selva oscura*, at midlife, and so do I. He discovers the gates of hell, which lead him at last to paradise; I just get out the shovel.

As the time approached for my mother's memorial service—a service my father had carefully planned in the days that she struggled to leave this life—it became apparent that none of us in the family had thought much about how to conduct a graveside service to take place earlier in the day. So I volunteered at the last minute to try to put something together. A couple of pastors that I knew reacquainted me with the traditional words of burial—words penned by Thomas Cranmer in *The Book of Common Prayer*, which he took over without too many changes from Catholic liturgy. These I adapted without too many changes myself, and I spoke them to our little circle in the moments before we placed a velvet bag of ashes into the ground:

> In the sure and certain hope of the resurrection to eternal life, through our Lord Jesus Christ, we commend to almighty God our mother, our wife, our sister, our friend, our mother-in-law, and our grandmother, and we commit her body to the ground—earth to earth, ashes to ashes, dust to dust. Blessed are the dead who die in the Lord, says the Spirit. They rest from their labors, and their works follow them.

Then we grabbed a shovel or two, some of us, and scooped the loose pile of dirt back into the hole on top of the bag. I read a prayer. We sang a hymn. And then we looked out over the cloudy reaches of the Willamette Valley from the damp slope of the country graveyard where we stood.

Earth to earth, ashes to ashes, dust to dust. So elemental. There was something about it that shocked me. This is my mother? A bag of ashes in the ground? And I am dropping dirt on top of her? But there was something pleasing about it as well—something good about helping my mother become a part of the earth again, whence she came and whither she returned. Just a few steps down the hill was the gravestone of her grandmother, buried there exactly a century before. I was helping to lay my mother to rest with her ancestors, with her own people. And that was good.

But according to the liturgy, that was not all. *Blessed are the dead who die in the Lord. They rest from their labors, and their works follow them.* They rest from theirs, obviously—my mother and great-grandmother. But it is my works that follow after: a whole trail to be made in their wake, reburying my lost mother with stroke after stroke of the shovel. I can't prove that this is so—that this is the literal impulse of my trail-making. But it seems plausible to me. My father often talks about the memorial service at their church that took place later that day. Many people spoke well of my mother, and that was very pleasing to him. But there is not much about that service that remains with me. What I most recall about the day is what it was like to bury a velvet bag of ashes, down deep among endless roots of poison oak.

At the close of the summer a poet from Oregon sent me a quote from Anaïs Nin: "Surely our parents give birth to us twice, the second time when they die." If this is true, my trail-building is not only a putting of my mother to rest. It is also a reenactment of my own birth. And a tangible action of rebirth. The first trail that each of us follows leads out from a shady recess and into the open fields of this world. We pause at the archetypal verge for a painful moment and move on. We leave our mothers at our birth and leave them again when they die. And again there is pain, a pain that is lessened by looking back and then moving on, finding a path, making a trail of blood behind us. This trail I am making is not just recapitulation. It is my beginning as well, the work of the living. It is as my mother would have liked it.

My mother had a twin brother who was the first to take me on a backpack trip in the Sierra: Graveyard Lakes, of all places. He died of cancer years ago as a relatively young man. When my mother was struggling with her own cancer, I dreamed of him. He had been a sickly child and was not a sturdy physical specimen as an adult. But in my dream his legs were rippling with muscle and vitality. He stood with a pack on his back and a quiet smile on his face. In the way that my uncle looked at me, I felt invited on the best hike I would ever take.

I took that dream as a hopeful sign and symbol of the resurrection. And there are other signs and symbols as well. One summer ago, a mountain lion and her cub were spotted coming down the canyon where the trail now is built. A few weeks before I began, they were seen again, the cub now grown into something like an adolescent. This makes us all a little afraid, and one neighbor of ours half-jokingly objected to the trail by saying, "Now you are making it easier for the mountain lions to come down to campus." But of course there is something lovely about these creatures as well. I like to think of them, of course, as mother and son. I never saw them as

I worked, but I want to believe that they saw me.

My mother grew up for the most part on an orange grove outside of Anaheim, California. She climbed the trees, chased the chickens, swam in the ditches, and, when she got older, hiked in the hills. Five months before I was born, she was stricken with polio. I knew her as a woman active in will, but not in body. She walked with a pronounced limp, often with the help of brace and crutches. In her last years she was almost wholly confined to a wheelchair. So even if she were still alive, she would not have been able to know my trail. I have a favorite spot on the path, however, where the sycamore grow wild and deep in the canyon below and even in August the sound of water trickling over stones can be heard. This is where the mountain lion and her cub are no doubt waiting for me, and this is where, someday, if this canyon is part of a new heaven and a new earth, my mother and uncle will come striding around the bend, inviting me to walk with them to higher ground.

Trail Maintenance

ONE SIZZLING AFTERNOON the summer after kindergarten, I brought out every one of my toys to our shaded patio and arranged them for all the kids in the neighborhood to enjoy. I pictured groups of friends contentedly assembling, some shaping Play-Doh, others coloring Mickey Mouse between the lines, others building orderly towns out of wooden blocks, through which yet others would lay tracks for a wooden train that snapped together. I spread out all of these things and more to give everyone sufficient room. Then, like the servant in the parable, I went out into the lanes and hedges of our block to compel the other children to this carefully prepared feast of recreational opportunity. To my surprise, I could persuade no one to come. Whether different ones of them had married a wife or purchased a yoke or two of oxen, I cannot now recall. But nobody was interested. I went back to my patio and wistfully surveyed the ruins of my social utopia. Then I put all of the toys away.

What interests me now about this memory is not the failure of the experiment. (As I recall, I did not lack for friends or brothers to play with. Nor did I mind playing alone.) What interests me is the impulse behind it. *These are my toys*, I wanted to say. *I want to share them with all of you. The more of you I can share them with, the happier I will be.* Nor did I imagine anyone fighting over these toys.

My generosity would somehow produce a perfect amity among all.

Some thirty years later my wife and I took twenty-four college students to England for a semester of study. This was a group that did not always get along. Some were very angry with me for weeks at a time, for reasons I found hard to discern. Later in the semester I discovered that a good many of these students had painful relationships with their fathers. Some had been physically abused, others abandoned. Others simply suffered an emotional distance. It became clear to me then that the anger directed at me by these students was anger that was transferred: in our *ad hoc* family for the semester, I got to be the father. Realizing this, however, did not make the situation much better. I still bore the anger of these students and slipped into a mild depression.

Back home after the semester was over, I sought the help of a therapist, who, as a good Jungian, told me to pay attention to my dreams. Some of the dreams that I could remember were disturbing, but one brought a sense of comfort. I was camped in an ancient hemlock forest with a whole variety of people: my wife and children and brothers and parents, my students and colleagues and old school friends, my teachers and pastors from the past, even authors dead and gone that I had read but never met. It was morning, and sunlight filtered through the hemlocks onto the moss and ferns and flowers. I helped everybody put on their packs, and we headed up a fresh, damp trail, ice axes firmly in hand. I was in the lead, setting a slow but purposeful pace, and everyone else was plodding along agreeably behind me. Through gaps in the trees overhead we caught a glimpse of a snowy volcano, white and gleaming and hopeful against the morning sky. It was understood that this summit was our goal for the day. We were going to climb it. But we weren't going to hurry. We would go slow, and enjoy every step, and make sure that everyone made it to the top.

That was my dream. My therapist told me it was a dream of healing and wholeness. A dream that brought everyone in my life together, in a setting that I dearly loved. As I think about it now, the dream may be a wilderness version of sharing my toys on the back patio. In both there is a generous impulse. Here are my toys; here are the mountains that I love. And in both there is community. Everyone is playing together peaceably; everyone is hiking in a humble kind of gratitude. There is no jockeying for position. I am in the front, but only to take care of the others. I felt none of the burdens of leadership in my wilderness dream. Only the joys of helping and of being helped.

I wonder: have I ever experienced this sort of thing in my waking life? I have been a college teacher for more than thirty years now. Has the classroom ever become this charmed space of community? There have been moments, of course. Moments I am sure that I have read a poem aloud in a way it deserves, or moments in which I have said something (unplanned) that seems to be the right word of understanding. Or, more importantly, moments in which I've really listened to something a student has had to say. For the most part, however, I have not experienced the sense of a shared gift in the classroom. I seem to grade a little too rigorously for the students' liking, and I am perhaps too much of an introvert to mount a charismatic presence. Every year, at graduation, my heart palpitates a little when the provost begins to announce the teacher-of-the year awards. But every year the awards are given to persons with different gifts than my own.

What about my years as a mountain guide, the real-life place that the dream came from? Again, there are moments of full connection, and plenty of them. Finding a Lewis's monkeyflower at the foot of a thundering waterfall, crossing a river safely in the North Cascades, summitting a Sierra peak that no one thought they could climb, dropping packs in the evening by a quiet tarn. The memories come crowding in. But I also recall the whining, the complaining, the sheer human recalcitrance of people who are asked to be a little cold, a little tired, a little hungry, a little blistered, a little dirty, a little bit bug-bitten. I also recall the sheer boredom on the trail of listening to adolescents discuss the latest movies, the latest sitcoms, the latest, greatest video games. There are no perfect group experiences. Only in dreams. Only in the kingdom of God, which is sort of now, but very much not yet.

And yet. What I want to write about is a trail I made last year along a creek on the edge of our California campus. The trail follows a ravine that is thick with brush and otherwise not very accessible. It is wild and shady down there, and almost completely out of sight of any of the college buildings or neighboring homes. With all of its branches, the trail amounts to about a mile of solitary walking—and, in the next couple of years, may grow by a mile more. It cost me seven months of slashing and digging to put the trail into place, and it still takes me several hours a week to maintain. When I built it, however, I was only thinking of myself. I was feeling hemmed in by the routine geography of the college campus and the adjacent faculty housing where I live. I wanted a place to wander alone, a place I could take my dog off the leash. Also, my mother had just died of cancer, and I felt a need to clear a new way for myself, to release the energy of my grief. So I threw myself at the poison oak and sure enough cleared a way.

I didn't advertise this trail. I didn't go door to door and ask the neighbors to share it with me. I even took a little pride in obscuring the places it started and stopped on public roadways. But, to my surprise, people began to find it. Perhaps they found the trail because they needed what I needed: a new way of being in the same place. Overworked faculty members and their maladjusted children. Stray students. Lonely visitors to the campus. And neighbors from beyond the campus. Lots of neighbors. Neighbors with dogs. Neighbors who had never had a kind word to say about the local college.

I didn't meet them all at once. They weren't in some long line, all hiking at my heels. But one at a time they'd find me working on the path and stop to thank me. Effusively. Some with strange tears in their eyes. A woman who, as a child, had suffered terrible abuse. Afraid of the woods, she'd decided this trail was friendly, and came to walk it every day. One morning, she told me, embarrassed, that she had created a private name for every section of the trail, every turn. Another woman, recovering from a painful divorce. She talked to me about Buddhist circumambulation and mandalas and other things I didn't know much about, but when she sensed my confusion she simplified and let me know the trail for her was a place to pray. And a man who told me, "This is the best thing that has happened to this neighborhood in thirty years." I found him spraying poison oak along the trail with a homemade brew. In fact, he extended one branch of the path to his back door so that he could have direct access.

So here is the irony of it all. My best gift to a local community wasn't really intended as a gift at all. I created a path for myself and discovered there is no such thing as a private trail. Though one person may carve it out, a footpath only continues to exist as communal expression. It is maintained not so much by one man's shovel and shears as by the feet of all who use it. It is like writing a book. One does so to satisfy one's own vision. But then, when the book is published, people read it or they don't. And if they don't, the book does not continue to exist, in any meaningful sense of that word.

Sometimes this communal reading and maintenance takes even more tangible forms. One part of the trail provides a leafy shortcut between the college track and the home of our college track coach, one of the most community-minded people I have ever known. His fourteen-year-old daughter is dying of a brain tumor, and the pain of this is etched on his face. He took her to the track by way of the trail once, when she could still walk a little, and he very proudly let me know. But now, as I write this, she is waiting at home to die. One would think a tragedy of this depth would preclude all outward vision. But one morning last month, our good coach had his whole team out on the trail with rakes and hoes and weed whackers, doing their bit to erase the encroaching growth of spring.

    I think too of the neighbor from beyond the campus who now patrols the poison oak with his hand-pumped brew. When I first met him on the trail, he eagerly asked for my email address. For several weeks afterward he peppered me with questions about tools to use, thistles to cut, stream crossings to rearrange. Then the emails stopped. I learned from a mutual friend that his twenty-two-year-old son had just died of a heart attack. I sent him a fumbling message of sorrow, and I have not seen him since. But when I do, we will be sharing the same path.

A Meditation for Ash Wednesday

MANY YEARS AGO THIS WINTER, I published my first novel. That was a proud day for me. I had a sense of maybe having achieved something of lasting significance. The novel sold reasonably well, made it into a second and third reprinting, and was even brought out again in mass-market paperback. But three or four years after it first came out, my publisher told me the novel was going out of print. There were a few thousand copies left over, and the publisher would either destroy them or send them to me for the cost of shipping. Of course, I couldn't bear to see my babies slaughtered like that, so I sprung for the shipping cost and my brother offered to store them in the hayloft of his barn in Oregon. As President Bush used to say, leave no child behind.

So, like the rich man in the parable, I had my harvest stored in my barn. Every summer I visited my brother in Oregon and visited my storehouse too, sometimes taking a box of books home with me. As summer followed summer, however, I noticed my treasure was showing some signs of wear and tear. It rains a lot in Oregon, and water had come through a leak in the roof and soaked some of the boxes through. Other boxes had holes chewed through the corners by mice, which also liked to digest the books themselves.

The occasional box was torn open by someone curious to take a copy, which was fine with me, but the rest of the books in the open box were left to collect dust and hay and pigeon droppings. Now, after years of careful storage, my literary legacy to the world doesn't look like much. Last I heard, my brother was using the last of the pulpy remnants to fire up his woodstove.

In the Renaissance they called this the problem of decay, the decay not only of our possessions but inevitably of our own lives. Shakespeare offers three solutions to this problem in his *Sonnets*. The first and most natural solution is to beget children who will survive us—children who will carry on some part of us when we are gone. But it doesn't always work that way. Just ask the parents who are bitterly grieving the loss of their children to illness, accident, or terror. As Shakespeare puts it in one of his plays, "Golden lads and girls all must, / As chimney sweepers, come to dust." The second way to solve the problem of decay, according to Shakespeare, is to be immortalized in a poem. For good literature lasts forever: "Not marble nor the gilded monuments / Of princes shall outlive this pow'rful rhyme." And that may work for Shakespeare to some extent, but as we have seen, it doesn't seem to be working for me. Shakespeare's third way to solve the problem of decay is probably the best way. It is to take part in a love that is bigger than we are—the kind of love that "alters not," that "bears it out even to the edge of doom"—a kind of love that can only be described as divine love.

In the gospel of Matthew, Jesus also describes for us our nagging problem of decay, and unlike Shakespeare he offers just one solution:

> Do not lay up for yourselves treasures on earth, where moth and rust consume and where thieves break in and steal, but lay up for yourselves treasures in heaven, where neither moth nor rust consumes and where thieves do not break in and steal.

It seems to me that Jesus' solution might be the same as Shakespeare's last one. To store up treasures in heaven is perhaps to devote ourselves to giving and receiving the unspeakable riches of God's love. Anything less is dust and ashes. Anything less is a rotting barnful of books. Heaven and earth will pass away, but the saving love of our Lord is forever.

So Jesus is reminding us that our many immortality projects never succeed in making us very immortal. They only succeed in making us feel motheaten, rusty, and ultimately ripped off. Ash Wednesday, with its visible sign of dust and ashes on our foreheads, is a forcible reminder of our own frailty and mortality and sinfulness. We don't like to remember those parts of ourselves, but on this day, it is literally rubbed into us. Scholars and monks in the middle ages would sometimes keep a human skull on their shelves to remind themselves of the brevity of this our life. A skull kept for this purpose was called a *memento mori*, which is Latin for "remember to die." Remembering the end of all flesh, these monks and scholars could better hold this world in contempt and strive to devote themselves to the eternal love of God.

The mark of ash rubbed into our foreheads can likewise serve as our own *memento mori*. But for us the mark is made in the shape of a cross. Thus it is not only a reminder of our own deaths, but also a reminder of the death of one who suffered agony in our place, the one who loved us and gave himself for us, the one who died that we might live, that we might have treasures in heaven. And we celebrate too, in the treasure of his flesh and his blood, the bread and the wine, the riches of his love for us.

Because of this miracle of his love, we can look on the ghastly skull of our own decay and say with the poet George Herbert:

> Death, thou wast once an uncouth, hideous thing,
> > Nothing but bones,
> > The sad effect of sadder groans:
> Thy mouth was open, but thou couldst not sing.

TO BUILD A TRAIL

•••

But since our Saviour's death did put some blood
        Into thy face;
    Thou art grown fair and full of grace,
Much in request, much sought for as a good.

For we do now behold thee gay and glad,
        As at doomsday;
    When souls shall wear their new array,
And all thy bones with beauty shall be clad.

•••

And when I read these lines by Herbert it seems to me that we ourselves, one with another, redeemed by the blood of Jesus, will be our own treasure in heaven.

Poems Lost, Poems Found

WHEN THE TEA FIRE CAME ROARING down the hillside, I was in my study putting the finishing touches on a poetry reading I was about to give that evening at Santa Barbara City College. But no—*roaring* is not the right word. For when my wife, Sharon, and I stood in the middle of Westmont Road and watched the flames advancing toward us on the wind, they in fact made no sound that we could hear. Aside from a hot rush of air in our faces, the night was eerily noiseless. It was rather like that scene in the film *The Perfect Storm* in which you think the brave little fishing boat has survived the weather, but then, all of a sudden, that huge killer wave advances, higher and higher, in complete silence. At that point your stomach drops in the theater with a sense of certain doom. That is how my stomach felt when we watched that quiet wave of flame come cresting toward us. I didn't know whether we had three minutes or thirty minutes to evacuate. But I didn't want to err on the wrong side of that estimate. And I wasn't much concerned with that poetry reading at City College anymore.

Unlike some people in Santa Barbara that night, we knew exactly where we were headed. We both worked at Westmont College,

Sharon as a nurse and I as a teacher, and we had already practiced our parts in a shelter-in-place program at the college gym. Sharon would be helping to care for hundreds of students in the gym itself, and I would be watching over neighborhood dogs in the men's locker room. So we put on our tennis shoes, shut our windows, collared our retriever, grabbed a few family photos, and backed our car out of the garage into a storm of falling embers. The gym was just a quarter mile away, on the other side of a ravine, and I remember wondering what would keep our car from being torched in the parking lot when we got there.

I also wondered if I had taken everything out of my study that I would have liked. For when I had entered that room again and surveyed its contents, I had stared blankly at my bookcase of several hundred poetry volumes, at a large stack of handwritten notes and poems that represented a year of sabbatical work, and at a manila folder of lit exams that I had been grading that day. I took the exams and left the rest. After all, I told myself, I couldn't rescue everything, and the house wouldn't really burn down, and I would need something to do while waiting in the locker room for the fire to pass.

Later I heard stories like this of people saving not the most valuable things but the things they had last touched. A woman who was frosting a cake put the cake on the front seat of her car and drove off, leaving her purse in the kitchen. A man who had just brought home a take-out meal from Taco Bell put all of the tacos back in the car and left everything else behind. Another man grabbed some empty suitcases and packed them full of sofa cushions. There is something about the human mind that does not work well in the face of fire.

After parting from Sharon in front of the gym and taping up most of the doors in the locker room to keep out the smoke, I tied the four dogs in my care to a wooden bench and sat among them correcting responses to Wilfred Owen and Flannery O'Connor in red ink. Every few minutes I snuck outside to see what I could of the conflagration. Ponderosas sent out flakes of fire on the wind. The redwood baseball stands exploded, and the tall stands of eucalyptus in the ravine were one long river of flame. On the other side of this Phlegethon, white-hot balls of incineration seemed to mark our faculty homes. *Oh, shit.* This, in fact, was the exact response of all four dogs in the locker room.

When, by midnight, the wind had slackened, and I walked back over to the neighborhood with a colleague, my stomach dropped once again when I saw that our house was gone. I think I literally collapsed on his shoulder. I remember staring into my study through a wall that was no longer there to where my desk would have been. The only thing I could see now was a filing cabinet radiating a red-hot glow. I thought about the files and files of poems inside it—some saved on my computer, some not.

So when I think about what I lost in that fire, I think most about the contents of my study. A month later, my friend David Starkey organized a benefit reading at City College to which people brought—to my amazement—twenty-six boxes of poetry books. Then former students showed up at our rented digs with several boxes more. As if I could actually read all of these! To have lost all of my own books was almost worth the experience of being literally overwhelmed by the generosity of friends and strangers in our community.

But the loss of the many poems I had drafted cut more deeply. These could not arrive in a box at the front door. I despaired of rewriting them, and for some time did not write much at all. But then, inevitably, I did. A poem here, a poem there, began to emerge. And—no surprise—many of them had things to say about the fire. The French believe we must suffer to be beautiful, and certainly pain is the price of art—not a welcome admission fee, but one that must be paid one way or the other. Suffering, in other words, is the deepening that makes art possible. Realizing this, I gradually came to think that I was getting those poems back—not the same ones I had lost, but perhaps better ones.

Two years after the fire, when my stomach had at last begun to find a safe and level place, I wrote a poem called "Lost and Found" that aims to express not only my longing for the things left behind but the natural and even ordinary way in which those losses may find repair. I'll let this poem be the last word here—though, of course, there is no such thing. Out of the painful silences of every fire, there is always the next word.

Lost and Found

If there is such a thing as found poems,
might there be lost poems as well?
And a place to find them after someone
turns them in? You would stop by a battered
desk in a corner, and there with your misplaced
set of keys, the scarf you dropped
in the parking lot, the pair of gloves left
in the restaurant, would be those stanzas of blank
verse you had to forsake when the embers
began to fall upon the roof of your house.
There would be the sonnet you sent
to that slender, acned girl from college—
your only copy—the girl that never wrote back.
Even the limerick you made up on the playground—
the one about your sixth-grade teacher
who frowned her way into retirement.
Every word that in Ariosto lands
on the backside of the moon, or in Milton
on that convex, windy shell of the universe,

the most precious, foolish things you have uttered,
would be handed to you by a woman with bright lipstick,
chewing gum and talking on the phone
with her husband, who is late getting off work but needs
to remember to pick up a loaf of whole-wheat bread
and a half gallon of non-fat on the way home.

By Any Other Name

I HAVE NEVER BEEN ONE TO NOTICE ROSES. I know the names of wildflowers by the score, particularly the alpine sort, and love to sit in mountain meadows counting petals and contemplating the sweet shine and attitude of shooting stars and Indian paintbrush. But roses. Roses are the poodles of the vegetable kingdom—domesticated, fretted over, too precious for their own good.

They have their uses, of course. When my mother turned seventy-five, my brothers and I rustled up that many red roses and surprised her with them—a whole cartload. And my own lovely wife, Sharon (the rose of Sharon!), seems to appreciate a dozen or so on special occasions as proof of my unwilted love. And then there was the time in college that a beautiful and breathy young woman, two years my senior, received a dozen anonymously. "Who could have sent these?" she asked in my presence. And I, who had not sent them, stammered and blushed. And thus began a rather interesting few weeks, until I was disastrously found out.

My interest in roses took a turn some years ago, however, when Sharon and I lost our home to a wildfire on the outskirts of Santa Barbara and temporarily rented a place in town near the old mission. We jogged to the mission with our dog almost every morning, which also meant jogging past our spreading municipal rose garden. There is something about loss that dulls the senses; as I recall, our stomachs were knotted with the trauma of the fire, and life passed as a distant dream. But there is also something about loss that allows one to notice things. And what I noticed about these roses is that they had names. Lots of names, announced for us on knee-high placards that lined the beds.

Rainbow Knockout, First Light, Wind Chimes, Buff Beauty, Hot Cocoa, Bishop Darlington, Red Coat, Child's Play, Innocence. *Nice*, I thought. Some, of course, were a little much: Sunshine Daydream, Perfect Moment, Honey Perfume, Tahitian Sunset, Mellow Yellow, Over the Moon. Overlooking these, however, I began to take a certain delight in reading off the names aloud and repeating them as I bounced across the grass after our golden retriever. There was a literary flavor to some: Clytemnestra, Penelope, William Shakespeare, Wise Portia, Fair Bianca, The Dark Lady. And there was, of course, a whole French Quarter: *Duchesse de Brabant, Etoile de Lyon, Marie Van Hautte, Monsieur Tillier, La Sylphide*, and—my favorite—*Beaute Inconstante*. Since I had never bothered to learn French, I ran around the garden mispronouncing these in Pig-Latin as I pleased: BE-U-TAY IN-CON-STAN-TAY, music to my ears alone.

Then there were the racier varieties—Playboy, Playgirl, X-Rated, Sheer Bliss, Sweet Surrender—reminding me that of all flowers, roses may be the most suggestively erotic. Before there was first base, second base, third base, and home, there was the French medieval *Romance of the Rose*, the whole point of which was to penetrate the rose in the center of the walled garden. It is no surprise, then, that many of the roses were simply named after women—or vice-versa: Rosaleen, Kathleen, Felicia, Brandy, Kristin, Cynthia—these the approachable girls next door when compared to the distant Madame Lombard or Lady Ann Kidwell. A surprising number of roses were named after real or imagined goddesses of recent times: Betty Boop, Marilyn Monroe, Audrey Hepburn, Elizabeth Taylor, Barbra Streisand, Sweet Diana, Maria Shriver, Julia Child. (*Julia Child?*) And some were even named after men—which, I thought, represented an almost complete failure of the imagination: William R. Smith, David Austin, Mr. Lincoln, Henry Fonda, Dick Clark. *Please*, I thought. Dick Clark may be many things. But he is not a rose. He has only faded like one.

How Are You, My Friend?

FOR THE YEAR AFTER OUR HOUSE burned down in the Tea Fire, my wife and I rented a condominium near downtown Santa Barbara. Our block was a mix of gentrified complexes and broken-down old homes. The street was shaded, the sidewalk buckled, and parking difficult to find. The condo had a roomy, covered front porch from which we could watch motorcycles motor by, but I don't recall that we sat down on that front porch all that often. Something about the trauma of the fire kept us restlessly pacing.

Our son was just a year out of college and back home from Los Angeles to work in a law office a few blocks away. A lover of cars, he had just bought a used Audi wagon to haul his drums from gig to gig. The perfect set of wheels for that purpose, he said. Our daughter lived a couple miles away with some friends, finishing up her own last year of college. This was our family—not counting the dog, which counted for a lot in those days. Years before, just after the 9/11 attacks, I took our dog to school for a week so the students could pet him during class. Similarly, in that year after the fire, our dog got a lot of attention. Or we craved his.

Right behind our condo was an old corner grocery store that

had just been taken over by an immigrant family from Syria. It had become more of a liquor store, actually. The grocery part was fairly sad. The bananas were speckled, the ice cream was chalky, and the milk perpetually past date. It was the kind of grocery store we only went to when we needed something at the last minute. But in the evening I would often walk the dog past the store and find the aging Syrian proprietor sitting calmly on the sidewalk, firing up a little stove to make some tea. Every time I walked by, he would call out, "How are you, my friend?"

I would say that I was fine and continue on.

The proprietor had two sons who worked in shifts. They were about the age of my own. Unlike their father, they were full of hurry and energy, as if through sheer force of personality their shabby corner grocery store could become the next Walmart. I often thought of them growing old in the fierce white light of those bottles of vodka behind the counter, their nimble hands passing change for packs of gum and packs of condoms. I wished that my students had half their hurry and energy; I wished that these two Syrian boys could go to college.

Late one spring evening, five months after the fire, our daughter woke us up with a call: our son had been in an accident in his Audi wagon. A very bad accident. He was in the emergency room, and we should get there, right away. When we found him behind a flimsy curtain, propped up in a bed and no longer conscious, he was still bleeding badly from a depressed skull fracture. He would need immediate surgery. Friends gathered through the night as he lay on the operating table, and then, in the morning, came word of likely recovery.

I do not remember everything of the weeks that followed, but here is something I do remember. My wife stayed at the hospital for several days and nights running, and I went home from time to time to walk the dog. One evening the dog and I passed in front of the corner grocery, and there was the old proprietor, sitting calmly on the sidewalk, firing up his stove for tea.

"How are you, my friend?" he said.

I stopped this time. I could not say I was fine, for I was not fine. Suddenly this Syrian man seemed to me the friendliest presence on the planet. I approached, and he very graciously arose. I told the dog to sit. And then I told the man about my son and his accident, about his crushed skull, and his operation, and how in the morning he had quietly opened his eyes and spoken to us. A miracle. But I told him how worried we were still, how the outcome was in no way sure, how my wife was still at the hospital and here I was, walking the dog.

The Syrian man stood very quietly and nodded. He listened to every word I said. "That is very hard, my friend," he said.

And then he said, "Please. Some tea, my friend."

I'd like to think I accepted his offer, that he poured me some tea in a little cracked cup, that we sat quietly side by side and drank together in little sips. But I probably just thanked him and left.

Night after night, however, I came back, walking the dog. And every time I passed by, if the Syrian father was sitting by the purr of his stove, he would call out, "How is your son, my friend?"

And I would tell him. Whatever the news might be, I would tell him. And my heart would well, every time. My heart, that little cracked cup.

III. Wonder

But of works of art little can be said; their influence is profound and silent, like the influence of nature; they mold by contact; we drink them up like water, and are bettered, yet know not how.

—ROBERT LOUIS STEVENSON

The Place

"THIS IS THE PLACE," SAID RUTH KERR. "This is the place the Lord has chosen for us." The year was 1945, and she had just driven through the sandstone entrance gate to the Murphy estate in Montecito. She and a small group of trustees were looking for a post-war home for Westmont College. According to Mrs. Kerr, they had found it.

By the time I got to Westmont some forty years later as a teacher of English, this story, like many others about Ruth Kerr, had gained the status of legend. You might even call it our creation myth. "'Let there be light'; and there was light," says the book of Genesis. "This is the place," said Mrs. Kerr. And this was the place.

Though I am not normally fond of people who get their way by claiming divine inspiration, for Mrs. Kerr I make an exception. This really has been the place. For over seventy years now, the former Murphy estate, with the addition of the old Deane School on lower campus, has been a gracious and fitting home for generations of our students.

The first time I saw the Westmont campus, however, I wasn't so sure that this was the place for me. A junior in high school, I had come to visit my older brother on my spring break. I stayed with him a night or two in his Armington dorm room, and during the day I sometimes went to his classes and sometimes wandered about on my own. In one class we sat outside Porter Theater in a small circle on the lawn with a young professor by the interesting name of Lyle Hillegas. I was surprised by how warmly he greeted me, by how much I felt included, by how intimate that circle felt in the sunshine out on the grass. I didn't know that education could be this personable. At the same time, I wasn't sure that something this personable could really count as education. Where were the brick buildings, the quadrangles, the ivy, the snow? These marks of a true education were conspicuously absent.

At the end of a day of wandering about on my own, my brother asked me, "Well, what do you think of the place?"

"I think a person could walk around all day, just saying hi to people."

"It's been done," my brother said.

Years later, reading *As You Like It* for the first time and reveling in what is perhaps Shakespeare's most delightful setting in all of his plays, I paused over what Celia says when she first enters the Forest of Arden: "I like this place, / And willingly could waste my time in it." For some reason I thought back to my first impressions of Westmont—to how powerfully drawn I had been to the place and, at the same time, how powerfully afraid I had been that I would waste my time there. As it turned out, I attended a pair of those bricks-and-ivy-and-snow institutions where education had a kind of grim certainty about it. And then I taught at one as well. When the invitation came to apply to Westmont, my feelings had long since started to change about what kind of place makes a good college.

These days, I spend most of my time in Reynolds Hall, a historic stucco building on lower campus that used to house the boys who attended the Deane School. There are six offices upstairs, mostly for the Modern Languages faculty, and six offices downstairs, for the English types. Each suite of offices surrounds its own sitting room with a fireplace. It doesn't rain all that often, but when it does, the students arrive dripping wet, and we have a fire of live oak going for them. I like to watch them crowding around the fireplace in their steaming clothes, laughing hard at nothing in particular, ready for class. On Friday afternoons our secretary serves tea for the English majors, and if it happens to be raining then, with a good fire in the fireplace, you might as well invite Lucy and Mr. Tumnus the faun to step out of the C. S. Lewis wardrobe at the side of the room. It is that cozy. In March the wisteria clothe the veranda in purpling vines. The windows and doors to the sitting rooms are flung wide, and the sun and the fragrance drift among us. As John Muir says, "One's body is all one tingling palate." We dart like swallows. We are that alive.

The sleeping porches for the boys of the old Deane School have long since been converted into the Reynolds classrooms. Each one has two full walls of windows that look out on a graceful lawn and the chaparral slopes of the Santa Ynez Mountains. This is handy for illustrating the Art-versus-Nature debate of the Renaissance. "Which do you prefer?" I ask. "Which is more beautiful? This open lawn with its curving path of cut stone, the product of human art and skill? Or that wilderness mountainside in the distance, the ceanothus in winter bloom and the ragged reach of sandstone cliffs—the natural landscape, unaltered by human hand?" The answer, of course, is both, and neither. The relatively ordered beauty of the campus would be claustrophobic indeed without the mountains rising behind it. After my first year of teaching here, I lit off into the hills on a pack trip and crossed paths with just eight people in eight days. I liked that. Last summer a mountain lion and her cub walked quietly down to Reynolds Hall, then just as quietly left. I liked that too. Recently, a woman in a garden hat also walked serenely past while pushing an elderly pug dog in a baby stroller. The dog was sitting nobly erect, nose in the air. In Montecito, art and nature still debate.

But I think it is the wild beauty of each new gathering of students on this side of all those windows that makes these classrooms what they are (though for some, of course—especially at 8:00 a.m.—the rooms fulfill their original function as places to sleep). Some professors much prefer to teach the specialized upper-division courses for majors. These courses have their obvious pleasures, but I also find satisfaction in teaching the introductory classes. Perhaps it is the evangelist inside of me that likes this challenge. To join a small roomful of freshmen and sophomores who are not at all sure that they like literature, or (more important) that literature likes them—what better place to start?

Fortunately, I can still remember what it was like to take my own first literature courses. How beautiful and confusing were the books we read! How inadequate I felt to comment upon them! How intimidating the English majors who seemed to know just what to say! When I first came to college, my idea of a good poet was Robert Service, and of a good poem "The Ballad of Blasphemous Bill." Why no one else shared this enthusiasm, I could not say. When asked to state the meaning of "The Waste Land," by T. S. Eliot, I read back to the elderly teacher the only line I understood: "In the mountains, there you feel free."

This same professor had a little habit that I noticed and I puzzled over. At the beginning of each class, he would open the text for the day with loving reverence, dividing the book like a loaf of bread and lowering the two halves with slow care. Hemingway, Faulkner, Pound, or Eliot—it didn't matter—they all received the same treatment. After a few weeks, I realized I had seen only one other book treated with such dignity: the Holy Bible. And a few weeks after that, I realized that what I was witnessing every day was a sacramental gesture, an integration of faith with learning, an acknowledgment that all truth is God's truth, wherever and in whatsoever form it is found.

I wish I could say I have carried out this gesture in my own classes with similar care and effect. But, alas, we now live in the age of throwaway paperbacks, which I toss about at the lectern with unceremonious abandon. In any case I seem to lack the physical patience and coordination to exactly imitate my professor. One thing that I seem able to do with some rightness, however, is to read a poem aloud. It is not a great gift, and it may not compensate for my many deficiencies as a teacher. (Quote from a student evaluation: "As it is, he putters around, often appears to lose track.") But I think that in reading a poem aloud, something close to the sacramental occasionally takes place. Grace can occur. Understanding. Those freshmen and sophomores sometimes get a wakeful look upon their faces. They lean in. They want more. They don't know what it is they want, but they want more.

Though I might choose any number of works to read with an introductory class, the poetry of John Donne and George Herbert, those seventeenth-century Anglican divines, always seems to find a place on my syllabus. Roughening up my voice a bit, I launch into Donne's "Holy Sonnet 14":

> Batter my heart, three-personed God; for you
> As yet but knock, breathe, shine, and seek to mend;
> That I may rise, and stand, o'erthrow me, and bend
> Your force, to break, blow, burn, and make me new.

I might pause here. I might ask why it is that the speaker calls on all three persons of God.

"The better to batter," says one.

"If it is, like a battering ram, he needs a whole army," says another. "An army of three."

They are a little surprised at themselves. They are getting this. The poem is not an impossible Rubik's cube after all.

"What are the three persons doing in the second line?" I ask them next. "Do you see three verbs in a row?"

They all nod. "Knock, breathe, shine," someone says.

"Might each verb describe the action of a different member of the Trinity? If so, which action for which member?"

"Knock," says a back-row dweller. "That's Jesus."

"Why?" I ask.

"'Knock, and the door will be opened unto you'?"

"Who's doing the knocking there?"

"Hmm," he says. "I guess we are."

"I know," says another. "'Behold, I stand at the door and knock.'"

"Who says that?"

"Jesus?"

"Where?"

"Revelations, maybe?"

"Revelation," I correct her. "But that's right. The risen Christ."

"Unlike a battering ram," says the boy who first brought it up. "Just knocking."

I am so delighted by this that I jump ahead to another question. "Do you see three more verbs in the fourth line?"

"Break, blow, burn," someone says.

"What's their relationship to 'knock, breathe, shine'?"

"Intense," says the surfer stretched out by the door. "Everything gets more intense."

"In what way?" I ask.

"He's not just knocking, he's totally breaking the whole door down."

"Like a battering ram," says the battering boy.

After a bit we get on to the next two lines of the poem: "I, like an usurped town, to another due, / Labor to admit you, but Oh, to no end. . . ." I throw my weight into the word *usurped*, then ask if anyone knows what it means.

"Like, to take over?"

"To take over wrongfully," I say.

"As in, 'Hey, usurped my Blenders,'" says a baseball player in the corner.

General laughter. He takes a bow, then retreats beneath his cap.

"Whatever it means," says a young woman in the front, "I just like the sound of it. It's fun to say. *Usurped*."

"Yes," I say. "Any other words that are fun to say in this poem?"

"*Batter*," says battering boy. "I can get my teeth into that."

"*Ravish*," says another. "It's the last word in the poem, and I like it. But I'm not really sure what it means."

"Anybody know?" I ask.

Silence. Hesitation. "Rape?" says someone in a whisper.

"That's right," I say. "Who wants to be raped in the poem, and by whom?"

"Donne," says the person. "By God."

"This is way too intense," says the surfer.

"Like a battering ram," says you-know-who—although this time he doesn't like the sound of it.

Next we go to a poem called "Love (III)," by George Herbert. I soften my voice considerably for the opening lines:

> Love bade me welcome; yet my soul drew back,
>   Guilty of dust and sin.
> But quick-eyed Love, observing me grow slack
>   From my first entrance in,
> Drew nearer to me, sweetly questioning
>   If I lacked anything.

"This is not John Donne," says one.

"What do you mean?"

"No one is getting battered and raped. That's what I mean. We're talking *love* here, with a capital *L*."

"But Herbert feels just as guilty as Donne," says another. "It says right there, 'Guilty of dust and sin.'"

"How can we be guilty of dust?" says someone else. "I don't get that."

"Mortality," her usually quiet seatmate says. "*Dust to dust.* Our reward for sin, maybe."

"Still," says the first speaker, "this is way different from Donne.

TO BUILD A TRAIL

A lot gentler."

"Keep going," I say.

"Sorry, that's it."

"Someone else?"

"Well, in Donne, he demands that God, like, totally attack him."

"And in Herbert?"

"In Herbert, God is like this wonderful host, or hostess—this really welcoming lady, maybe, who has you over to her house—who demands—no, just invites—invites you to sit down to a meal."

"Who's right?" I ask.

"About what?"

"About God," I say. "About what God does."

"They're both right," says the quiet young woman. "But I think Herbert is more right."

"For you, maybe," says the baseball player forcefully.

"So maybe different ones of us experience God in different ways? Maybe we need both poets?"

"In the green," says the surfer.

"In the green?" I say.

"Right inside the tube," he says. "The very best part of the wave."

I have had some version of this discussion more than a time or two. Perhaps I have idealized it a little bit, combining some of the better moments from different classes. But the spirit of such conversation, the potential of it, is always there—in the sacrament of the spoken poem, in the way that Love bids us gently or batters us with sudden force. As a teacher I am the handheld dummy for ventriloquist poets who projected their voices long ago. I have only to say the words, and I am not the one who says them. I am merely a medium, and beyond that, merely a witness to what happens in the magic circle of a many-windowed classroom.

And so much happens among my students that I never get to witness. In a Renaissance literature course some years ago, we read all thousand pages of *The Faerie Queene*, the longest poem in the English language. One pair of roommates in the class read the entire work aloud to each other, week by week, canto by canto, in the privacy of their room. Another pair of students drove to the same funky coffee shop each Thursday night and composed poems, side by side. Yet another started a club that wrote by flashlight on the beach. And this is not to mention the unfathomable mystery of solitary reading and writing. Who can calculate what happens when a student is fully and completely absorbed in George Eliot's *Middlemarch* and discovers at the very end that "the growing good of the world is partly dependent on unhistoric acts; and that things are not so ill with you and me as they might have been, is half owing to the number who lived faithfully a hidden life, and rest in unvisited tombs." Or think of the same student hard at work on a paper at midnight, discovering the metaphor that makes her next sentence sing. There is a hidden life of literature. "Sing, Heav'nly Muse," says John Milton. But the muse is not a heavenly host, it is not a choir. It is more like the wind of the Spirit, faithfully heard by one ear at a time.

One spring I took a carload of students to the university across town to hear the Palestinian-American poet Naomi Shihab Nye. She was sparkling and gracious in her reading, and as we drove back to Westmont, expressing our enthusiasm to each other for Nye's work, one student, who was due to graduate in a few weeks, quietly said, "That was the best experience of my whole time in college." Who can say what had transpired within her? What miracles of reception take place every day that no one ever shares or speaks of?

Of course, we invite a good number of scholars and writers and artists to our own campus to present their work to our students. (Naomi Shihab Nye has even arrived of late.) The most distinguished venue for our guest presenters is Hieronymus Lounge in Kerrwood Hall, the dark-panelled parlor of the great house that once belonged to the Murphy family but was purchased for us by Ruth Kerr. Her portrait hangs just over the fireplace, behind the lectern. She wears a farsighted, mysterious expression, lips pursed, as if reserving judgment on what is happening here these days. I joke sometimes when introducing a visiting poet that if Ruth Kerr really and truly likes a poem, her face will blossom into approval. In his poem "The Tyger," William Blake asks of the Creator, "Did he smile his work to see?" I sometimes wonder the same thing about Mrs. Kerr. Does she smile her work to see? Or our work, rather? The eyes of her portrait gaze across the carpet and couches of the lounge to the windowed doors, slightly ajar, that open onto a giant redwood planted in the circled lawn. There is a faint, clean smell of eucalyptus in the air, and, beyond the reach of the redwood tree, chaparral shines far and far to sandstone summits. This is the place, Ruth Kerr. This is still the place that the Lord has chosen.

Assessment

Ninety-five percent of those who read this poem
will experience a sense of wonder. The other
five percent are wondering how to arrive
at this statistic. For evidence is what is needed.

Otherwise the poem will never gain accreditation,
and no one will want to attend. We could ask
for a show of hands, but some of the readers are related
to the poet, and nothing surprises them anymore.

If the poem is read aloud, carefully trained monitors
could be placed in the audience to count
the number of mouths agape in stupefaction
or in slumber. How many persons are leaning

forward, eager for the next word? This is an angle
our monitors can quietly measure, pulling
from their back pockets a gathering hush
of collapsible wooden protractors.

If all else fails, electrodes may be placed
on the correct lobes of the brain—

TO BUILD A TRAIL

or for certain lines, on the genitals.
The results will be graphed on a table of outcomes

in the report that forever after must be stapled
to the body of this poem. Perhaps you have seen
a great blue heron lumbering down a pond for takeoff,
its feet entwined in dripping skeins of lily pads.

The morning sun illuminates the strain of the wings,
the encumbrance of roots and petals
dragging their weight across the dark brown of the water.
The bird never rises. No wonder.

A Letter to the Faculty

25 March 2014

DEAR COLLEAGUES,

On Friday, while explaining a proposal about assessment in a faculty meeting, John Blondell experienced a slip of the tongue and coined the term Assessmont College. This got me to thinking that there may in fact be two different institutions—Westmont College and Assessmont College—each with its own tasks, its own identity, its own ethos.

At Westmont College, faculty teach and learn with their students and with one another in spontaneous, flexible, and trusting ways. There is a confidence that what is being learned is good but measureless. There is even a sense that if what is being learned were not measureless, it would not be worth learning.

At Westmont College, faculty do research with their students and offer extra tutorials for the sheer love of learning. They are not overly concerned with technique, nor are they concerned with efficiency. These students and faculty did not come to Westmont College because they believed that education would, could, or should be an efficient process. If they believe anything, they believe that curiosity, love, and wonder always take circuitous paths toward understanding.

This brings us to Assessmont College, which is quite a different place. At Assessmont College, the words *wonder* and *understanding* are not allowed on course syllabi because *wonder* and *understanding* do not constitute measurable outcomes. At Assessmont College, the task is constantly to evaluate how much learning is taking place, and of what sort. While in Westmont College there are three academic divisions, in Assessmont College there is only one—the division of social sciences. Each course is considered an ongoing social science experiment; each professor is mainly understood to be a social scientist whose primary job is not so much to teach his or her classes as it is to constantly mine them for usable data.

At Assessmont College, a culture of trust between colleagues is replaced by a so-called culture of evidence. That is because, at Assessmont College, we lose confidence that what we teach and what we learn is in fact measureless—that our learning is like Shakespeare's star "whose worth's unknown, although his height be taken." If we cannot graph it, if we cannot chart it, if we cannot fit it into a rubric, it doesn't count—and it doesn't exist.

At Assessmont College, we do not have time for extra research or tutorials with our students, because we have another assessment meeting to attend. We do not have time to deepen our own acquaintance with our disciplines, because we have more assessment data to organize. We do not have time for that walk or lunch or dessert with our students because there is another survey to fill out. And yet, paradoxically, Assessmont College proclaims that it is all about efficiency, ideal product, desirable outcomes. At Assessmont College, the utilitarians become entangled in their own utility.

On Thursday, in a faculty forum, Gregg Afman shared with us

his vision of a cadaver lab at Westmont College. This sounds like a laudable goal, and I commend his persistence in trying to achieve it. But let me borrow this notion of a cadaver lab as a metaphor. A cadaver lab, as I said, may well be a helpful part of Westmont College. But at Assessmont College, that is perhaps all that the entire institution will become—one giant cadaver lab.

Envision, if you will, the student body, the body of the faculty, the bodies of our disciplines, all laid out on rows of tables in every building on our campus—all laid out for an endless process of dissection. These bodies are no longer alive—they no longer live and move and have their being—because, as William Wordsworth reminds us, "We murder to dissect."

Immeasurably yours,

Paul Willis
Professor of English

The Sixth Chapter of Acts

NOW DURING THOSE DAYS, when the disciples were increasing in number, the Hellenists complained against the Hebrews because their widows were being neglected in the daily distribution of food. And the twelve called together the whole community of the disciples and said, "Please take a few moments of your time to fill out this important survey." And the survey was given. And the survey was taken. And 86.5% of the disciples completed the survey.

Then said the twelve, "It appears that 13.5% of the disciples have not filled out this important survey. They shall be called outliers, and shall be taken where they do not wish to go. And the 13.5% fell down and died. And great fear seized all who heard of it. The young men came and wrapped up their bodies, then carried them out and buried them.

Then said the twelve, "It now seems good to us to select a consultant to interpret the results of this important survey. A commission of seven will be appointed to evaluate the merits of the various consulting agencies available and then to report back to us. For it is not right that we should neglect the word of God in order to wait upon survey results."

What they said pleased the remaining 86.5% of the community, and they chose Stephen, who was full of the spirit of his MBA, together with Philip, Prochorus, Nicanor, Timon, Parmenas, and Nicolaus, a graduate of Antioch Polytechnic Institute. But once the seven were named, a dispute arose among the 86.5% as to the cultural bias of the commission. For it was noted that all seven were Hellenists, and none were Hebrews—and that the Hellenists were bound to be prejudiced in their consideration of various consulting agencies in favor of their brother and sister Hellenists who had brought the original complaint.

And the twelve said, "Let us form a Commission of Fairness in Matters of Cultural Orientation to which we may refer this matter. And let us call it the CFMCO, for short." And so a second commission of seven was formed—three Hellenists; three Hebrews; and one who, as a result of an operation, was a resident of Trans-Jordan. And after deliberation, fasting, and prayer, the CFMCO appointed themselves as a substitute commission for the evaluation of the merits of various consulting agencies for the eventual selection of a consultant to interpret the results of the important survey.

And the CFMCO met regularly, on alternate Tuesdays, at a restaurant of their choice. And they recommended the Du Gud Consulting Agency located in Alexandria. And a collection was taken to fund the first-class round-trip galley fare for a consultant, who arrived from Alexandria and insisted on five-star accommodations. And many portions of food designated for Hebrew (and possibly Hellenist) widows were re-routed to provide 24-hour room service for the consultant.

And the consultant said, "I would like to provide an overview of the results of your important survey, but unfortunately the instrument was poorly constructed, and did not take into account the possible limitations of the respondents." So after a farewell banquet with the CFMCO, the consultant returned to the port, accompanied by the twelve. And there was much weeping among them all; they embraced the consultant and kissed him.

Then, before boarding his galley, the consultant declared in the hearing of all, "Before constructing a revised version of your important survey, you must first identify a measurable survey learning outcome that you would like to attain. In this effort, it is important not to be swayed by the merely aspirational. For example, do not hope to ascertain how many widows of which sort are receiving sustenance, for that is a subjective matter of some indeterminacy, as we do not live by bread alone. A much better starting place, within the scope of your survey, would be to quantify the exact number of Hellenist widows who eat with their left hands."

This pleased the twelve greatly, and they made arrangements for the consultant to visit them annually in order to gauge their progress in attaining their measurable survey learning outcomes. They returned to Jerusalem emboldened to reconstruct their important survey in a way designed to attain data-driven decision-making for all future eventualities. The 86.5% greeted the twelve with joy, at which time the twelve excused themselves to an upper room for their weekly long-term planning retreat, during which they fine-tuned their survey instrument.

At the end of their retreat the important survey was given again. And it was found that the respondent sample of Hellenist widows had dwindled considerably. And none remained who ate with her left hand.

The Garrison Keillor Koan

EVERY ONCE IN A WHILE, Garrison Keillor came to town to deliver one of his trademark monologues. There he would be, alone on stage in his dark suit and flaming red socks, meandering from story to story and leading us, both at the beginning and near the end, in a medley of old folk tunes and hymns. How did he do it—spinning these tales *ad infinitum* out of his head? I could not tell. The man was a gentle genius.

Of course, my wife and I had listened to him on the radio for nigh unto forty years. He was as much a part of our marriage as anyone or anything we could remember. *A Prairie Home Companion* mixed with baking smells in our kitchen on Saturday afternoons, and Sharon in particular started almost every morning with a five-minute visit to *The Writer's Almanac*. One Sunday morning she insisted I listen too, even though we were late for church, and very impatiently, I consented, wading through a list of birthdays of this author and that author before being completely blindsided by a reading of one of my own poems.

So, the last time he came to Santa Barbara, on a rainy winter afternoon, we made the trip down to the old theater to see what he was up to now. It was the weekend of the inauguration of Donald J. Trump, but that turned out to be too much of a fat pitch. He didn't mention Trump at all. But I'm getting a little ahead of myself. The surprise of the afternoon, for us, was that when we walked into the foyer, just ten minutes before the show, Garrison Keillor was standing by the door to the theater proper, relaxed as can be, just chatting with a few folks. So I thought, well, this is our chance to say hello, and after waiting our turn, we did.

Garrison Keillor is an extremely tall man, and when he gave us his attention, he did so from on high, it seemed. And, too, there was something paradoxical about the way he looked at us, making concerted eye contact and, yet, not making eye contact at all. But we quickly introduced ourselves, and I thanked him for reading that poem of mine. He wanted to know which one it was, and I described it, but he couldn't bring it to memory. I told him I taught creative writing at Westmont College just up the hill, and at the beginning of most of my classes I played *The Writer's Almanac*, and that the students were especially interested—inspired, even—by the stories he told about how people became writers.

Instead of saying "Thank you" or "That's nice to know," he broke in and said, with an oddly definite emphasis, "You beat up on those kids. Beat up on them."

I must have laughed, thinking he was making a joke. But he leaned in hard and said it again, his eyes and voice quite serious: "You beat up on those kids." And again, a fourth time. *"Beat up on them."*

And then he was gone, whisked away by the theater host to reappear just moments later on the stage. And I was left to wonder, as I have since, what exactly he meant to tell me.

There may have been some clues in the opening moments of his monologue. He told about a niece of his (real or imagined) who had gotten pregnant and given birth, how he and his wife had taken them in, both the young woman and the baby. The father of the child was a graduate student who couldn't quite make up his mind about taking on his new responsibilities. Once in a while he came for dinner, but the fellow hardly ever spoke up, and when he did, it was only to mumble. "Diction!" Garrison Keillor thundered. Here was a young man, he said, who couldn't speak, who couldn't write, and yet was on the point of gaining a master's degree in communications. As for his niece, her lips and cheeks and nose and ears had so many piercings that she looked as if she had tripped and fallen face-first into a tackle box.

And so it went. The first half hour of the monologue was spiced with similar trash talk about hapless failings of hapless millennials—of whom there were very few in the room.

Could it be? I wondered to myself. Could this man I had thought of for most of my life as a genial uncle actually be, in his heart of hearts, a cranky old man? Was I simply being deputized—since I still had some influence, since I was still in the classroom—to take revenge on a whole generation of shifters and slackers? Certainly there was nothing to gain by simply being mean to students. I did not want to be mean to my students. Of course, I wanted to hold them accountable (and I thought that I did), and perhaps that's all he had meant. Perhaps he had wanted to remind me to remind them that writing is very hard work, not simply a matter of being inspired. Or maybe he really had been kidding—both with me in private and with his audience in public. Which was it? Humor can be so slippery! But if I had been given a mandate, not an over-the-top pleasantry, what was it, exactly, and how could I possibly carry it out?

Sharon's theory was that Garrison Keillor is the kind of person who doesn't tolerate compliments. On the way home, she said, "Remember when he was on the phone with Barack Obama last summer—that phone call during his last show—and Obama praised him for all those years on *A Prairie Home Companion*? He couldn't just say thank you. It's like he wanted to change the subject. You were saying something nice to him, and he couldn't take it. He turned it right around on you."

My wife is very good that way—socially observant. But if he were just deflecting a compliment, why deflect it so hard and so long? And in just that way?

The next morning I told my fiction writing students what Keillor had said, and that turned out to be a mistake. I tried to turn it into a lesson about the many complications and contradictions inherent in human character. They just winced at me, perturbed.

A few days later I told my provost, and he just laughed. "Keillor's a quick study," he said. "It only took him a few moments of conversation, and he had you pegged for a patsy in the classroom."

Now it was my turn to wince.

Two months later I told my story to a poet-teacher friend who had spent some time with Garrison Keillor. "What you have to know," she said carefully, "is that Garrison Keillor is very funny onstage but not that funny in person." She thought what he had said to me was very strange—but was probably an expression of an actual frustration of his. Her brow was furrowed as she spoke. "No one really teaches by beating up on people," she said. "That never works."

So I think about this little koan that Garrison Keillor dropped in my lap. In spite of all the exegetical help I've received, I haven't come to enlightenment yet. And sometimes I wish he had never told me what he told me. For the only person I have beat up on, subsequently and consequently, is myself!

But now I wonder if maybe, just maybe, it was merely a matter of transference. Donald Trump had just become our president two days before. Garrison Keillor had decided not to say a word about it that afternoon. But his sadness and anger had to land somewhere. And why not on the next generation, the very ones who needed to become good and caring and wise enough to avoid repeating the national mistake we had just made? They needed to be taught well. And fast.

If that's all that was behind his prompting, his strangely urgent exhortation, I'm fine with it. But I would prefer to walk softly, and not carry somebody else's big stick.

What's a Laureate to Do?

WHEN THE MAYOR OF OUR MODEST TOWN, herself a former English major, called to say that I had been selected as our next poet laureate, I felt both honored and perplexed. Honored to be chosen, of course, but perplexed as to how to perform this very visible office. My habits as a poet were to wander off into the woods, contemplate the poison oak, and then put pen to paper, arriving at stray ruminations that might or might not interest the average working citizen. But a poet laureate—surely a poet laureate must have something civic-minded to say.

It wasn't long, however, before I realized I was not alone in this quandary. At the time, a full thirty-seven cities and counties in the state of California had poet laureates of one sort or another. And that is not counting the many state laureates throughout the country, in addition to our revolving series of national poet laureates. Just a week after I had joined this burgeoning field (albeit at the junior varsity level), I happened to be introduced to a daughter of the current Librarian of Congress. The Librarian of Congress is the person who vets and supervises our national poet laureates, so this daughter knew something about them.

"How are you feeling about your new role?" she asked me, and I could tell she wanted to know.

"I'm not really sure," I said. "It seems so—public."

"Exactly," she said. "It can be quite a burden." She went on to say that for most poet laureates at the national level, their year or two of service is a disconcerting experience. "The only one that I know of who really enjoyed it is Billy Collins."

Great, I thought. If only I were as clever and as extroverted as Billy Collins.

Ready or not, however, I started in. I organized my fair share of community readings and workshops, and I showed up pretty much wherever or whenever asked in order to grace some public occasion with a poem. Quite often, I would be asked to write a poem specifically for a given purpose. (The first assignment for my successor was to celebrate a new wastewater treatment plant.) In spite of my secret diffidence, I never really questioned these prompts, choosing to believe in my scrappy efforts to fulfill them. That is, until the day I was invited to dinner with the poet Jane Hirshfield.

In keeping with Jane Hirshfield's respect for Zen poetry, the hosts of the dinner provided us with an exquisite Japanese meal. With no forks or spoons or knives, of course. Just chopsticks. Three simple things I cannot do, and, yea, even a fourth: whistle a tune, snap my fingers, blow bubbles of any kind with Bazooka bubblegum, and, yea, transport food from plate to lips with a pair of chopsticks. So the others were having a serene time of it, a perfectly Zen culinary experience, while I flailed away at every bite of nothing but air.

That's when Jane Hirshfield asked me, "What do they have you do as a local poet laureate?"

"It's a poet lariat, actually," I said. "I just write cowboy poetry."

"No, really," Jane Hirshfield said, not even smiling.

"Well," I said. "I organize readings and workshops, read poems for civic occasions, and, when asked, write poems on assignment for special events."

That's when she got animated. "They make you *do* that?" she said. "You *let* them make you do that? You let them treat you like—like some sort of short-order cook?"

"Well, sure. It's part of the job," I said, tweezing my chopsticks like a pair of twirling batons.

"I would *never* do that," she said.

I reminded her then that I had seen a poem or two from her very own hand that was actually written for a wedding, but she didn't give much ground. For her, the writing of an occasional poem was a violation of the muse.

A few weeks later, I was having lunch in Portland with the poet laureate of the state of Oregon, Paulann Petersen. I told her about my conversation with Jane Hirshfield and asked her how *she* felt about writing poems on demand. Paulann became very earnest. She said it was her privilege and responsibility to write a poem both to and for a given group at their special request. "It's not always my best work," she admitted. "But it's a valuable and necessary way to participate in my community." She went on to tell a story, the details of which I have now forgotten, about reading a poem to the entire Oregon state legislature. What I do remember was how moved she was to have had this experience—and not moved in a way of how important it made her feel, but in a way of how important it was to be able to share a poem in that setting.

What you must know, Dear Reader, is that I greatly admire both Jane Hirshfield and Paulann Petersen. On this question of writing the occasional occasional poem, however, I have come to side with Paulann. And here are some of the reasons why, rooted in my own recent experience.

First, let me elaborate the question. If I am writing a poem on assignment for a given community, does this enhance or injure the poem? Does my membership in community help me or keep me from saying what I need to say? How can I write an occasional poem that is both publicly appropriate and personally authentic? These, for me, are the real issues.

Early on in my term of service, I was asked to write two different poems for the tenth anniversary of the September 11 attacks. One was to introduce a performance of the Mozart *Requiem* by the Santa Barbara Choral Society at a large Presbyterian church. I had several months to work on it, and I carefully studied the text of the *Requiem* while composing the poem, listening to various recordings as well. I came up with something nuanced and sophisticated, I proudly thought, full of knowing allusions to the Latin mass.

The other 9/11 poem was written at the last minute at the request of a local fire captain. The fire and police departments were holding a morning ceremony on the steps of the county courthouse to honor the many first-responders who had lost their lives in the tragedy. Would I write a poem for the ceremony? The crowd would be surrounded by members and veterans of all our armed services. There would be a twenty-one-gun salute, a flyover of jets from a nearby airbase. I would be one of the few on the courthouse steps who were not in uniform. I took a deep breath, and said yes.

To write the poem, I thought of researching a good bit more about the 9/11 attacks—for there is always more to learn—but in the end I did no further research at all. For I realized that all I could think of were those many firefighters climbing the stairwells of the World Trade Center—the same image that all of us have deeply imprinted on our minds. And I thought too of my audience: honest folks who don't generally read much poetry. What I came up with was something almost embarrassingly simple and repetitive, a call-and-response poem that owes maybe a teeny bit to Tennyson's "Charge of the Light Brigade," likewise written in response to a national sorrow. The poem is called "FDNY"—the initials, of course, for Fire Department New York.

FDNY

And did they climb those stairs?
    They did. Oh yes, they did.
        Oh yes, they did.

And did they find their duty there?
    They did. Oh yes, they did.

And when those towers fell, what then?
    What did become of them?
        What then?

They kept on climbing. Yes, they did.
    With all their heart, with all their will,
        They kept on climbing still.

And are they climbing even now?
    And are they climbing now?

Oh yes, they are. They're climbing there.
    On stairs and towers everywhere,
        In boots and hats and heavy fare
            They keep on climbing through that air
            To do their duty there.

And do they still, with right good will?
    Oh yes, they do, for me, for you.
        They keep on climbing for they care
        To do their dusty duty there.

And shall we bless them full and fair?
    We shall, oh yes, we shall, we shall,
        We shall bless them everywhere.

TO BUILD A TRAIL

of the meadow underneath the bell towers,
desperately in need of their blessing.

I took comfort in knowing they had been there
for a long time, shadowing others in their search
for certainty, for something in their lives that would stay.
Oh, I know those towers crumbled in an earthquake in 1925,
and whatever had preceded them was reduced
to rubble in 1812. And I also know that the Chumash
were not altogether grateful to be herded into these precincts
and forced to build that fern-covered dam on the creek.

And the long abuse of those boys at the school—
I know about that too. But driving home from work
that winter, I often chose the longer route
that brought me down the canyon to that graceful turn
around those towers rising above the rusty leaves
of sycamore in the last of the sun, my gaze
falling across the lawn to the tile rooftops of our city,
the ocean beyond, the islands glinting like a promise.

And I would think of those many friars, most of them
so patient and humble, so full of faith, so dedicated
to those who came to place their burdens on the warm stone
of these steps that lead out from that sanctuary
to the rest of this beautiful, suffering world.

IV. Gratitude

Literature is a form of fondness for life.

—GEORGE SAUNDERS

My First Summer in the Sierra

IN THE SUMMER OF 1974, just finished with my freshman year at Wheaton College, I found myself leading hiking and climbing trips on the north boundary of Yosemite National Park. Though I had visited Yosemite Valley for a week of scrambling two years before, this was my first full summer in the Sierra. I found that I certainly liked the place, that I felt at home here: the deep blue skies, the granite peaks, the shapely domes, the meadowy canyons, the shining streams—it was all very unlike the rain-soaked Cascades that I had grown up with in Oregon, and altogether very unlike the dull Chicago suburb of Wheaton, where I had felt trapped for the school year. So when I found this passage in a book by a previous visitor to the park, I felt he was speaking for me:

> We are now in the mountains and they are in us, kindling enthusiasm, making every nerve quiver, filling every pore and cell of us. Our flesh-and-bone tabernacle seems transparent as glass to the beauty about us, as if truly an inseparable part of it, thrilling with the air and trees, streams and rocks, in the waves of the sun,—a part of all nature,

> neither old nor young, sick nor well, but immortal. . . .
> How glorious a conversion, so complete and wholesome
> it is, scarce memory enough of old bondage days left as
> a standpoint to view it from! In this newness of life we
> seem to have been so always.

This previous visitor was John Muir, who grew up in a Disciples of Christ family in Scotland and Wisconsin and came to California at the age of 30, hungry for a place to call his own. He found this place while herding sheep in Yosemite during the summer of 1869, and, late in life, after founding the Sierra Club and fathering several national parks, he revised his journal for publication in 1911 as *My First Summer in the Sierra*.

This was the book that I read in my own first summer in the Sierra, and it gave me words to fit my experience in ways that continue to unfold. As a boy, Muir had been made to memorize all of the New Testament and much of the Old, and as a result his own prose is resonant with biblical phrases. Because of the abusiveness of his father, however, Muir seems to have abandoned a specifically Christian theology by the time he came to California. (In the passage above, the "glorious . . . conversion" is to the mountains, "old bondage days" seem roughly equivalent to regimented life in the city, and "newness of life" is that generally found in nature.) At the same time, Muir retained a deep sense of a loving God who is expressed most powerfully and intimately in the beauties of the wild. For this he is ecstatically grateful in his writing. He sees about him "A terrestrial eternity. A gift of good God." I, in turn, felt grateful for his fervent witness.

As I led my charges through the Sierra that fine summer, there was one passage I often repeated to myself:

> From garden to garden, ridge to ridge, I drifted enchanted, . . .
> gazing afar over domes and peaks, lakes and woods, and
> the billowy glaciated fields. . . . In the midst of such beauty,

pierced with its rays, one's body is all one tingling palate.
Who wouldn't be a mountaineer!

Notice that Muir does not end with a question mark, as one might expect, but with an exclamation point. He is that sure of God's goodness as expressed in the creation.

He has made me sure as well.

Three Old Ones

Sonnet 104
—William Shakespeare (1564–1616)

To me, fair friend, you never can be old,
For as you were when first your eye I eyed,
Such seems your beauty still. Three winters cold
Have from the forests shook three summers' pride,
Three beauteous springs to yellow autumn turned
In process of the seasons have I seen,
Three April perfumes in three hot Junes burned,
Since first I saw you fresh, which yet are green.
Ah, yet doth beauty, like a dial hand,
Steal from his figure, and no pace perceived;
So your sweet hue, which methinks still doth stand,
Hath motion, and mine eye may be deceived;
    For fear of which, hear this, thou age unbred:
    Ere you were born was beauty's summer dead.

I did not read Shakespeare's *Sonnets* until I was in my mid-twenties. Then I read them all at once, in astonishment, in an old and empty classroom at Gonzaga University in Spokane, Washington. It was summer, and the classroom was cool and shadowed, and I somehow had all these words to myself. I couldn't get over how inevitable they were, how effortless they seemed. And yet, of course, they were the result of great artistry.

I especially liked "Sonnet 104" because of its intimacy, beauty, and anguish. "To me, fair friend, you never can be old" is not only a great line for a birthday card but also a good example of how a poem can address another person on easy and natural terms. Sometimes, when drafts of my own poems feel vague and ungrounded, I address them to a specific person, and suddenly they come to earth. The earnest wonder of the speaker for the beloved—that is what makes the poem work.

And then I noticed how, in the process of saying he has known the beloved for three years, the speaker creates a litany of the seasons that is an object of earnest wonder itself. "Three April perfumes in three hot Junes burned" become markers not only of time but also of beauty, a natural beauty in which the beloved participates. Shakespeare is not writing a "nature poem" per se, but he evokes the beauty of nature as a matter of course—it is always available to him, whatever else he is on his way to explore.

The third quatrain probably tripped me up the first time I encountered it. But, as with most Shakespearean similes, this one is not that hard to figure out. Just as an hour hand on a clock cannot be seen to move with the naked eye, the beauty of the beloved cannot be seen to diminish. But the hour hand *does* move, and the "sweet hue" of the beloved likewise will depart. Shakespeare is up to his old "problem of decay," the ancient challenge of death and time to human sensibility.

In some sonnets he solves this problem by recommending that the beloved beget children. In other sonnets he aspires to participate in a divine love that transcends death. In still other sonnets he adopts the classical solution of immortalizing the beloved in a poem. That is his solution here, but he announces it in a heartbroken way, which is part of what makes this particular sonnet so interesting. Out of confidence that his poems will last, he addresses the "age unbred." But what he has to tell us does not engender much hope: before we were born, the most beautiful person ever to have lived was already dead. And it is the way this sonnet comes to a bump on the word "dead" that is so disconcerting. It is as if he is getting a little tired of the premise that the beloved can live on in the contents of his poem. "Sonnet 104," I think, is a halfway house between the easy optimism of "Sonnet 18" ("Shall I compare thee to a summer's day?") and the fervent hope of the eternal in "Sonnet 116" ("Let me not to the marriage of true minds").

In the midst of all this seriousness, Shakespeare is also having a lot of fun. How else to account for the line "when first your eye I eyed"? Every once in a while, I encounter a poet who believes that a public reading should be a solemn exercise. All I can say is that such a poet has Shakespeare to contend with. In his plays, he routinely mixes comedy with tragedy, tipsiness with sobriety. He has given us the mirror up to nature, the true range of who we are as human beings. He helps us laugh in the face of death and shed a tear in the presence of beauty. Sonnet 104 is a précis of his lifelong method. For me, in my own way, it is a method well worth imitating.

To Blossoms
—Robert Herrick (1591–1674)

Fair pledges of a fruitful tree,
    Why do ye fall so fast?
    Your date is not so past
But you may stay yet here a while,
    To blush and gently smile,
        And go at last.

> What, were ye born to be
>> An hour or half's delight,
>> And so to bid good-night?
> 'Twas pity nature brought ye forth
>> Merely to show your worth,
>>> And lose you quite.
>
> But you are lovely leaves, where we
>> May read how soon things have
>> Their end, though ne'er so brave;
> And after they have shown their pride,
>> Like you a while, they glide
>>> Into the grave.

For an Anglican divine, Robert Herrick may not be the most spiritually sincere of poets, but he awakens me to the beauty and the pathos of nature as few other writers do. For the wistful spirit of *carpe diem*, he is unsurpassable. "To Blossoms" is one of his many poems about flowers that fade. He addresses the fading flowers so simply, so sweetly, and so sadly that I find myself reading this poem over and over.

In the first stanza, he personifies the blossoms as girls that blush and smile, much as he does with those rosebud-gatherers in "To the Virgins, to Make Much of Time." In the third stanza, their leaves become leaves of a book in which we read our destiny. In the end, like the flowers, all of us "glide / Into the grave," resting at last in that poignantly shortened final line.

The American poet Stanley Kunitz dated his beginning as a writer to the moment when, at age fourteen, upon hearing a teacher read Herrick's poem "Upon Julia's Clothes," he put up his hand and said that he liked the word "liquefaction." In "To Blossoms," I would put up my hand for the word "glide." There it sits, gliding off the end of the line, willing for its vowel to soar far and wide for as long as we like. Wordsworth makes the point in his Preface to the *Lyrical Ballads* that poets use common terms, but use them in uncommon ways, giving them weight and wonder by where exactly they are placed. And so here. In a sense the entire poem serves as a set-up for this one word—"glide"—that is uncommonly situated.

What I also notice about this poem is the way in which the blossoms are directly and intimately addressed. Flipping through my own poems, many of which are "about nature," I see that I also sometimes do this. I'll title a poem with a species name, even adding the scientific name in parentheses, and then speak to the plant as if it can hear. In the poem "Sierra Juniper," for example, I begin, "Your clustered berries, dusky blue, / offer themselves to the sun again / in the twisted reach of your close- / pressed leaves." Do trees have standing? This was a famous legal question raised a generation ago. If you can talk to them in person, I suppose they do.

The Dawning
—George Herbert (1593–1633)

    Awake sad heart, whom sorrow ever drowns;
        Take up thine eyes, which feed on earth;
    Unfold thy forehead gathered into frowns:
        Thy Saviour comes, and with him mirth:
            Awake, awake;
    And with a thankful heart his comforts take.
        But thou dost still lament, and pine, and cry;
        And feel his death, but not his victory.

    Arise sad heart; if thou do not withstand,
        Christ's resurrection thine may be:
    Do not by hanging down break from the hand,
        Which as it riseth, raiseth thee:

A Meditation for Good Friday

WE ALL KNOW THE STORY of Barabbas—his release from jail which sealed the warrant of death for Jesus. Matthew calls him "a notorious prisoner"; John, "a bandit"; Mark, one "who had committed murder." Growing up, I thought of Barabbas simply as a very bad man in these conventional terms.

Now that I am older, I find that the gospels tell us more. Mark actually identifies Barabbas as a rebel, one of a group of rebels "who had committed murder in the insurrection"—as if we were to know what insurrection this was. Luke, from a greater historical distance, describes Barabbas as "a man who had been thrown into prison for an insurrection started in the city, and for murder." Barabbas, in other words, is something more than your average thug. He seems to have been a political figure—a Zealot, perhaps, feverishly working to undermine Roman rule. In our day, we might call him a terrorist.

To think of Barabbas as a political terrorist is to rethink his significance to the gospel. I was told, growing up, that the story of Barabbas is a parable of our fickleness toward Christ. Five days before Good Friday, the people honored Jesus with palms and hosannas. Now they allow the chief priests to reverse their loyalties. The acclamation of "Blessed is he who comes in the name of the Lord" becomes the condemnation of "Crucify, crucify him!" The story of Barabbas, I was told, is the story of our inability to love long and love well, of our strange willingness to kill our prophets. As Peter says to his countrymen in the Book of Acts, ". . . you asked for a murderer to be granted to you, and killed the author of life."

I cannot say that I disagree. The story of Barabbas is of course a measure of our lack of faithfulness to Christ. But I now think it is also a measure of our faithfulness to Barabbas. If we realize Barabbas as a terrorist, we also realize our commitment to terrorism, legal or illegal, as the time-honored way of getting what we think we want. To ask for Barabbas is thus not at all an unnatural thing. A man imprisoned for taking part in an insurrection is bound to be a political hero, and there are bound to be people working for his release. To ask for Barabbas instead of for Jesus is to ask for the sort of messiah we know and love and fervently believe in. We have been asking for him ever since. His names are Osama Bin Laden, Yasser Arafat, Fidel Castro, Ariel Sharon, George Washington, Henry V. His names are also Bill Clinton and George W. Bush, Barack Obama (all those drones!) and Donald Trump, for all politics—all politics—are inextricably rooted in violence.

Understood in this way, Barabbas is a measure not only of our choice but also of Christ's chosen path. Jesus, as we know, could have been a political messiah, and was in fact expected to be at every turn. When shown all the kingdoms of the world, however, he rejected each one—even the United States of America (which, I presume, he could also see in a moment of time from that mountaintop). "My kingship," he told Pilate, "is not of this world; if my kingship were of this world, my servants would fight . . . ; but my kingship is not from the world." And so Jesus chose to disarm Peter, and to heal the ear of that unfortunate servant in the garden. Jesus chose to lead his followers in prayer, not in insurrections. He chose to be murdered, not to murder.

A MEDITATION FOR GOOD FRIDAY

According to some manuscripts of the Gospel of Matthew, Barabbas' full name is Jesus Barabbas. Pilate asks the people, "Whom do you want me to release for you, Jesus Barabbas or Jesus who is called the Messiah?" The coincidence of names holds further irony when we note that *Bar-abbas* means "son of the father." Jesus Barabbas, fully considered, is anti-Christ, the Christ that Jesus could have become and the one that we most obviously prefer.

The good news, I now think, is that it is Christ's preference, and not our preference, that really counts. Herein lies the irresistible symbolism of the exchange: Jesus the Christ dies in place of Jesus the terrorist; Christ goes to the cross, Barabbas goes free. Barabbas is the first of all of us who might have said, "While we were yet sinners, Christ died for us."

For here is the miracle. Every day, we choose the terrorist, Jesus Barabbas. But Jesus the Christ, Prince of Peace, chooses us. It is Jesus, not Pilate, who releases Barabbas and all his followers.

A Century Past "The Soldier"

WHEN I BEGAN TEACHING at Westmont College in 1988, I met a woman at church who had also taught in our English Department. Her name was Dorothy Docking, and she was very old and spry. More importantly, she was from England. Her brother was an automaker, she once told me. Back in the thirties, he had asked her what they should call a brand-new model he had designed. Dorothy had just been reading *The Jungle Book*, by Rudyard Kipling, so she said to her brother, "Why not call it a Jaguar?"

Dorothy was good for stories like that—and for all I knew, they were true. So I shouldn't have been all that surprised when one morning, after the service, while people were out talking in the sunshine on the patio, she came up to me and said, "I know how Rupert Brooke came to write 'The Soldier.'"

"Really?" I said. For this was of genuine interest to me—of greater interest than Jaguars. "The Soldier" is a sonnet from the early months of World War One. Its blend of sheer patriotism and ethereal religious nostalgia had taken England by storm, and the poem was read aloud from virtually every pulpit in the country. Today it is usually put on display in anthologies as an example of

An Evening with the Palestinian Poets

ONE RECENT OCTOBER, a pair of Palestinian poets—Fady Joudah and Gassan Zaqtan—stopped by Westmont College in Santa Barbara to read their work. They were at the tail end of a two-week tour, sponsored by the Poetry Foundation, which had included stops at Harvard, Yale, Columbia, and the University of Texas. Thanks to our adjunct professor Greg Orfalea, an Arab-American writer himself, we had managed to borrow them from UCLA. When Greg introduced the poets in the pit of our science lecture hall, packed to the brim, he said it had been an eventful and emotional tour—that the students at Brandeis had collectively broken down in tears. Well, I thought, does that mean that we are supposed to cry too? Far be it from us to be outdone by the Ivy League.

I don't know about you, but I am contrary like that.

I know as much about the Palestinian-Israeli conflict as the next person—which is to say, not as much as I might. And going into that afternoon's reading, I knew exactly one Palestinian poet—the ever-gracious Naomi Shihab Nye. But I didn't know what to expect from the Palestinian men. The elder poet, Ghassan Zaqtan, stood up front with a sort of noble weariness to him. The younger, Fady Joudah,

And the villages:
Children packed in a hut
Then burned or hung on bayonets,
Truck tires

Anchoring acacia limbs as checkpoints.
And only animals return:
The monkeys dash to the road's edge and back
Into the alleyways,

And by a doorstep a hawk dives
And snatches a serpent—your eyes
Twitch in saccades and staccatos:

This blue crested hoopoe is whizzing ahead of us
From bough to bough,
The hummingbird wings

Like fighter jets
Refueling in midair.

    Joudah's poems serve as witness not only to the pain of his people, but also and more immediately to his experiences over the last ten years with Doctors Without Borders in places like Darfur. Later, at dinner, he referred to an essay about this group that had tried to defuse the heroic aura surrounding these altruistic physicians. "Doctors Without Borders is not about saving the world," he said. "It is about acts of common decency. That's the best we can do. That's all we can do."

    In the question-and-answer session following the reading, when asked about a possible solution to the Palestinian-Israeli conflict, Zaqtan stated unequivocally that the only hope was a single state. Joudah was more pessimistic. The solution, he said bitterly, if indeed it ever came about, would take place long after his lifetime.

AN EVENING WITH THE PALESTINIAN POETS

When challenged on this by a colleague at dinner, who suggested that history provides more than a few surprising examples of accommodation between enemies that occurs sooner than one might imagine, he flew into something of a rage. He was tired of condescending remarks like this from outsiders, he said. What we needed was to move beyond the myth of the nation-state—the myth that a people only matter if they form a nation-state. "We need to see that for what it is—as just a myth," he said.

"But there's no such thing as 'just a myth,'" I found myself interjecting. As the song says, I don't know much about history, but now we were verging on literature. "We live and breath by myths," I added. "There's no such thing as mythlessness—of getting beyond them. They can be re-shaped. They can be challenged. By great writers sometimes. Shakespeare questions the myth of revenge in *Hamlet*. Milton turns the myth of the warrior-hero on its head in *Paradise Lost*."

He looked at me and waved his hand. "Who reads Milton?" he said.

Later, of course, Greg diplomatically mentioned to me that Fady and I may have been making the same point.

Oh well.

At the end of this remarkable evening—and it was remarkable, in uncanny ways I can scarcely describe—Fady Joudah apologized for what he feared was his rudeness and threw his arms around me as if I were his long-lost friend. I went home thinking about this and other acts of common decency, our uncommon words that still go with them.

For when our food had been brought to the table, Greg had asked me to say a prayer. Taking a deep breath, I had instructed everyone to join hands, and then gave thanks in the name of Jesus. Fady had looked at me and laughed. "Ghassan is used to that," he said. "His wife is a Palestinian Christian."

My Date with Mary Oliver

SO. THE POET MARY OLIVER was coming to town—or to the local university, rather—and the head of their arts and lectures series, Roman Baratiak, called me up and asked if I would introduce her at the reading. Would I ever. An honor, I told him. Her lithe and lovely stanzas of encounter with the natural world, stair-stepping down the page, were among my very favorite moments as a reader, moments in which I often forgot to envy her skill and simply sank into the words—words that made me more of the kind of grateful and attentive person I wanted to be. And that's what a good poem is for, right?

Roman told me to arrive a half hour early so that Mary Oliver and I could chat a bit before she went on. "To establish some rapport," he said. So I got to the lecture hall by 7:30 p.m., intro in hand, eager for my little chat. But the stage manager came out and told me that our guest poet was still at dinner, would get here soon—that I should have a seat in the house and someone would get me when she arrived. So I took a seat near the front as the large hall began to fill.

At a quarter of eight she still hadn't shown. Then ten to eight. Then five to eight. The lecture hall was full by now, ripe with

TO BUILD A TRAIL

the proper depths of my pocket. And in response to these questions in hand, we did find out, among other things, that Shelley's "To a Sky-Lark" ranks among her favorite poems, and that "It is the east, and Juliet is the sun" is among her favorite lines—"the naked power of metaphor," as she put it.

To Mary Oliver's relief, I ended our conversation when, by the glow of my trusty wristwatch, twenty minutes had elapsed. To my surprise, I did not regret a single fumbling word I'd said. And, to my un-surprise, I treasured each and every word that Mary Oliver had uttered. Afterward, people told me, "You looked so spontaneous up there!"

Well, duh.

And I still haven't washed the smoke from my jacket.

Notes

Dedication

    7. "I sing of times trans-shifting . . . ," Robert Herrick, "The Argument of His Book," *Hesperides* (1648).

Epigraph

    11. "We get no good . . . ," Elizabeth Barrett Browning, *Aurora Leigh* 1.702-09 (1856).

Into the Wilderness

    14. "Why are we letting the data geeks . . . ," qtd. in Haley Sweetland Edwards, "Should U.S. Colleges Be Graded by the Government?" *Time* 28 Apr. 2014, p. 35.

    15. "The freshness, the freedom . . . ," Robert Service, "The Spell of the Yukon," *Collected Poems* (New York: Putnam's, 1940), p. 4.

I. Curiosity

    17. "Stories are not multiplication tables . . . ," Daniel Taylor, personal communication.

Remembering Those We Forget

30. "Girl in the front row . . . ," William Stafford, "At Liberty School," *The Way It Is: New and Selected Poems* (Graywolf Press, 1998), p. 90.

31. "standing with," cf. Kim Stafford, *Early Morning: Remembering My Father, William Stafford* (Graywolf Press, 2002), p. 39.

Here, Mr. Hoerth

39. John Warwick Montgomery, *The Quest for Noah's Ark* (Bethany Fellowship, 1972).

40. "As it was in the days of Noah . . . ," Luke 17:26, King James Version (KJV).

Hitchin' a Ride

47. "We're all bastards . . . ," Will Campbell, *Brother to a Dragonfly* (Continuum, 1977), p. 220.

II. Love

57. "Poetry is a response . . . ," Wallace Stevens, *Collected Poetry and Prose*, ed. Frank Kermode and Joan Richardson (Harcourt, 1963), p. 913.

To Build a Trail

59. "He being dead . . . ," Hebrews 11:4, KJV.

65. "In the sure and certain hope . . . ," adapted from *The Book of Common Prayer* (1552).

66. "Surely our parents give birth . . . ," Anaïs Nin, *The Diary of Anaïs Nin*, Vol. 5: 1947–1955, ed. Gunther Stuhlmann (Mariner Books, 1975), p. 184.

A Meditation for Ash Wednesday

76. "Golden lads and girls . . . ," William Shakespeare, *Cymbeline*

NOTES

4.2.

"Not marble nor the gilded . . . ," William Shakespeare, "Sonnet 55," *Sonnets* (1609).

76. "bears it out even to the edge . . . ," William Shakespeare, "Sonnet 116," *Sonnets* (1609).

"Do not lay up for yourselves . . . ," Matthew 6:19–21, Revised Standard Version (RSV).

77. "Death, thou wast once . . . ," George Herbert, "Death," *The Temple* (1633).

III. Wonder

93. "But of works of art . . . ," Robert Louis Stevenson, "Books Which Have Influenced Me," *Letters and Miscellanies of Robert Louis Stevenson: Sketches, Criticisms, Etc.* (Scribner's, 1898), pp. 303–04.

The Place

95. "This is the place . . . ," qtd. in Nancy L. Phinney, "Westmont College: 75 Years," *Noticias: Journal of the Santa Barbara Historical Museum* 14.1 (2012), p. 10.

96. "I like this place . . . ," William Shakespeare, *As You Like It* 2.4.

97. "One's body is all one . . . ," John Muir, *My First Summer in the Sierra* (Houghton, 1911), p. 153.

99. "Batter my heart . . . ," John Donne, "Holy Sonnet 14," *Songs and Sonnets* (1633).

101. "Love bade me welcome . . . ," George Herbert, "Love (III)," *The Temple* (1633).

103. "the growing good . . . ," George Eliot, *Middlemarch*, Book 8, "Finale" (1872).

"Sing, Heav'nly Muse," John Milton, *Paradise Lost* 1.6 (1667).

Acknowledgments

Antler: "Three Old Ones" (as "Sonnet 104," "On Robert Herrick," and "Throwback: George Herbert's 'The Dawning'")

Books & Culture: "A Century Past 'The Soldier,'" "An Evening with the Palestinian Poets," "Here, Mr. Hoerth," and "My Date with Mary Oliver"

The Broadsider: "On the 225th Year of Mission Santa Barbara"

Covenant Companion: "My First Summer in the Sierra" (as "In the Midst of Beauty")

The Cresset: "Gumdrops," "Hitchin' a Ride," "Into the Wilderness," "The Shirt on Our Backs," and "Trail Maintenance"

English Journal: "Assessment"

Every Day Poems: "By Any Other Name"

OE Journal: "To Build a Trail"

The Other Side: "Epiphany at Patsy Clark's" and "A Meditation for

Good Friday" (as "Barabbas")

Rolling Coulter: "Common Ground"

Saint Katherine Review: "How Are You, My Friend?"

Santa Monica Review: "Piano Lessons"

Say This Prayer into the Past (Cascade Books): "Lost and Found"

Tahoma Literary Review: "Remembering Those We Forget" and "Salvatore"

Westmont: "FDNY" and "The Place"

• • •

"Assessment" and "FDNY" also appeared in *Say This Prayer into the Past* (Cascade Books).

"Common Ground" also appeared in *Visiting Home* (Pecan Grove Press), *Writer's Almanac*, and *The Barricades of Heaven* (Heyday Books).

"On the 225th Year of Mission Santa Barbara" also appeared in *From Glory to Glory* (Poetry in the Cathedral), *Say This Prayer into the Past* (Cascade Books), and *What Breathes Us* (Gunpowder Press).

"Salvatore" also appeared in *Getting to Gardisky Lake* (Stephen F. Austin State University Press).

"To Build a Trail" also appeared in *The Bubble*.

Thanks

I AM GRATEFUL TO ALL KINDS of folks for their assistance and inspiration. My former student Melanie Smedley was the first to brave the barrancas *sans* trail—and write about them—thus giving me the courage to someday follow in her footsteps, shovel in hand. My former colleague Heather Speirs helped me to notice the essay as a literary form that was quite literally under our noses. Since we were always grading these things, why not make them fun? Of all the editors who are implicitly thanked in my acknowledgments, John Wilson deserves my special appreciation for his curious faith in my nascent abilities, not to mention his heroic shepherding of the late, lamented *Books & Culture*. I do want to thank the Provost of Westmont College, Mark Sargent, for a strategic sabbatical in which I had this book in mind; he has borne all my protests of the culture of assessment with wit and considerable wisdom. And my heartfelt thanks to my WordFarm publishers and editors, Andrew and Sally Sampson Craft, for sticking with me all these years and taking such pains with my work. Finally, I wish to thank my entire family for loving (and for humoring) me, especially my wife, Sharon. To her I dedicate this book.

About the Author

PAUL J. WILLIS is a professor of English at Westmont College and a former poet laureate of Santa Barbara, California. He is the author of *Bright Shoots of Everlastingness: Essays on Faith and the American Wild*, named by *Foreword* magazine as the best essay collection of the year from an independent press. He has also published five volumes of poetry, most recently *Getting to Gardisky Lake* and *Deer at Twilight: Poems from the North Cascades*. Also set in the Cascades—or at least a mythic version of them—is his eco-fantasy novel *The Alpine Tales*. Learn more at *pauljwillis.com*.